The Roots of Evil:

A Postmodern Exploration of the Unintended Consequences of Civilization

By

Evan Longin, EdD

Table of Contents

About the Author

Evan Longin has a long history of confronting the unintended consequences of civilization. From his earliest days in the fields of psychology and education, he has worked with institutions and individuals who are struggling with the difficulties of society. As a doctoral student at Boston University, he was a fellow with the Division of Legal Medicine, helping incarcerated youth. As a postdoctoral extern at the Nathan Ackerman Family Institute, in the early days of family therapy, he became aware of the limitations of psychotherapy theory. Longin taught for over twenty-five years at Salem State University, where he was a professor of graduate counseling. He has practiced clinical psychology for over forty years. He also has worked as a consultant to school systems in the Salem, Massachusetts area; cofounded-- the Salem Center, a training center for postmodern practices in therapy; and was a principal at Artsbridge, an organization dedicated to bringing Islamic and Jewish children together in Palestine and Israel. He has three children and five grandsons. They, of course, taught him the most about curiosity and love.

Abstract

The following discussion is a basic presumption that evil is not an entity but rather a perspective created by the powers in authority to maintain control of the community. The book's basic proposition is that evil happens when four factors converge:

1. Binary thinking (i.e., "us versus them")
2. Control of information
3. Simplistic solutions to complex situations
4. Power over behavior

The book further proposes that the two basic genetic predispositions of humankind—love and curiosity—are often threatening to authority. It also reviews and deconstructs ideas and beliefs often taken for granted in our Western culture, analyzing from historical and contemporaneous contexts situations where evil has materialized. Finally, it demonstrates how the same macrocultural factors can bring about evil as an unintended consequence of education, religion, and psychotherapeutic practice. By offering postmodern practices as an alternative to modernism, this book attempts to demonstrate how modernism is stultified and unable to bring about new possibilities in a rapidly changing world.

Outline

I. The basic presumption is that evil is not an entity, nor does it reside within the internal functioning of an individual. Rather, it is a perspective created by the powers in authority to maintain control of the community. In certain circumstances (e.g., mental illness), it is a particular individual's misguided efforts to assert themselves over another or others to gain and/or maintain power or control. The basic proposition of this book is that evil happens when four factors converge:

    1. Binary thinking (i.e., "us versus them")

    2. Control of information

    3. Simplistic solutions to complex problems

    4. Power over behavior

II. Examples of evil situations that meet the expressed criteria include the following:

    1. The Vietnam War

    2. The Iraq War

    3. The violence between Palestinians and Israelis

    4. The violence between Catholics and Protestants in Northern Ireland

    5. Apartheid and/or segregation

6. The Catholic Church reformation, including removal and persecution of those who believed in alternative Gospels

7. Inquisitions by the Catholic Church

III. The antidotes to evil are love and curiosity, two internal forces that are programmed into our genes. However, the complete list of core values that lead to moral behavior is as follows:

1. Curiosity is the good and natural state of humankind. All learning and mastery are rooted in this instinctual condition of our being.

2. Previously held beliefs and narratives should be deconstructed. It is important to comprehend the derivation of ideas in the historical context in which the ideas were or are developed.

3. Ideas are evolutionary, always open to new definitions and possibilities.

4. Collaboration between people is useful and preferred to any conversation that is limited and/or dominated by any particular group or ethos. This can lead to a more complete understanding of situations, the development of more complex solutions, and the sharing of information and points of view.

5. An individual can hold several ideas, perspectives, philosophies, and/or points of view simultaneously.

6. All discussion and dialogue can—and should—take place in a loving, affirming manner.

Dedication

This book is dedicated to two men who helped shape my life. My father, Joseph Longin, as those who knew him, challenged ideas and beliefs often taken for granted. He was a loving yet disciplined man. He demanded that I always think about the unintended consequences of our actions.

Paul Franklin M.D. was a giant of a thinker and yet warm and compassionate. He escaped the holocaust and subsequently learned that his family was exterminated. While being my supervisor he taught me to listen to people's pain and never minimize it. "It is not our job to determine which person's pain is legitimate. Our function is to witness their pain and honor them for facing it."

Acknowledgement

In order to have written a book that attributes Love and Curiosity as the antidote to Evil, one has to have had experiences that have supported those ideas. My life has been enriched with a myriad of opportunities supported by my family to learn about the benefits of these virtues. Watching my children Melissa, Todd and Brian, and then my grandchildren; Kyle, Ryan, Luke, Nate and Will, develop over time, I have watched the innate force of curiosity drive them forward to success in the world. They along with my wife Philippa have taught me repeatedly the benefits of deep and uncompromised love.

This book could not have been created without the support and technical know how of many people in my life. Deb Nathan was always there when my technical ability to work my computer was inadequate. She from time to time, was supported by my son Brian and my grand sons Ryan and Luke . I can't enumerate the number of times my son Brian and my daughter in law Erin rescued pieces of my manuscript from cyber space. It is unimaginable to think that my grandsons actually have more computer skills then I. Unfortunately, I never received an education in computer technology and I am a luddite at heart. My long time secretary Lorilyn Navarro was always available over the course of my teaching and practice to assist me with collating my materials.

I must give a shout out to those people who I drove insane by sending them jumbled and unreadable texts. They would tell me that I kept repeating myself and I would shrug, thinking really! Finally I read the materials that I sent out only to realize the text was not collated properly and parts of chapters would repeat and be out of order. Thank you Jack and Linda Weltner and my brother Howard.

My efforts at writing this book were enhanced by the friendship and knowledge of my two dear friends Liz Solar and Ken Kolpan. They read my drafts and encouraged me forward. Liz , in particular, is an author herself and introduced me to people in her life. One extremely important individual she introduced me to was my editor Sara Letourneau. She took my interesting and valuable ideas and turned it into readable book. I am deeply indebted to this talented woman.

It is important that I also acknowledge the many students and interns I have taught over the last twenty-five years They have given me the opportunity to develop these concepts and challenged me along the way to demonstrate the validity of my thinking. There have been so many students and colleagues that I cannot mention them all. However, I want to particularly recognize my colleagues over the years at the Salem Center. This center was responsible for developing many of the ideas that I practiced and talked about in the book. These people included Marjory Roberts, Steve Gaddis, William Blain-

Wallace, Deb Nathan, Henry Zapata, Cheryl Schilling, Sarah Malloy, Carol Anne Hale and Kristin Cordy.

Endorsements

Richard Bourne Ph.D., J.D, Professor Emeritus, Department of Sociology, Northeastern University, Former Associate General Counsel, Children's Hospital Boston: Dr. Longin has written an important and provocative book on evil: its definition, extent, causes, and consequences. Using numerous examples from history and the present, he emphasizes four conditions necessary for its existence and, thankfully, what behaviors are able to lessen its destructiveness.

Andrew Menard J.D. Executive Director, Strategy and Innovation, Johns Hopkins Radiology: Drawing on decades of clinical experience, Dr. Longin explains how war, societal polarization, oppression, inequity, and more are byproducts of civilization. But he contends that such evil is not inevitable. Human nature offers the seeds of healing that we can consciously cultivate if we recognize the power of our innate curiosity and our capacity for love.

Deborah Nathan LMHC ATR, Adjunct Faculty Lesley University, Founder of Artsbridge Institute: The Roots of Evil is a must-read for anybody that wants to understand the many challenges facing our world today and how we arrived at such polarities in our society. This book asks us to question our beliefs regarding the concept of evil and the institutions that may be inadvertently contributing to so many of the conflicts societies are currently facing.

Liz Solar, Host of the Embark podcast., Voice Actor, Storyteller at Acts of Revision: What is Evil and how do we overcome it? Evan Longin examines its roots, as well as our individual and tribal perceptions of evil. Through the lens of his considerable experience as a psychotherapist, Longin cites several factors, including abuse of power and binary thinking, which provide fuel for incendiary acts on and against each other. A clarion call to a long-overdue national conversation.

Introduction

During the George W. Bush administration, the period when this book was originally conceived, the issues leading to evil were taking hold both in the U.S. and its allies. Since then, the urgency of facing the coming darkness has increased exponentially. The concerns of the Bush years—misleading information, power over behavior, and binary thinking—multiplied during Donald Trump's presidency, which was dominated by lying and mindless, ignorant thinking. The ideas contained in this book are even more pertinent today than they were during the Bush years.

The entire American democracy is at stake. Donald Trump—both as president and during his post-presidency—has become a catalyst for the germination of evil. Much like villains of the past, he seeks power over the community and has been willing to distort reality. And like other recent despots, he has a personality that can rev up the masses and spin lies and untruths. Could we ever have imagined QAnon before he emerged onto the national political scene? It is little wonder that his answers to complex problems are simplistic at best and destructive at worst.

Trump has advocated for the building of a wall to keep out immigrants, proclaiming that the Mexicans will pay for it. He separated families at the US-Mexico border and detained children for months. He has also suggested that the COVID-19 virus was no more problematic than the flu and that we could treat it by injecting ourselves with disinfectant. Furthermore, he has pitted US residents into a struggle of "us versus them," denied science, and ignored the existential threat of our times: climate change.

This book is meant to clarify how evil becomes present in our community so easily. Furthermore, it is meant to demonstrate how fragile our democracy is.

As a psychotherapist, I have listened as families struggled, trapped in a cycle of discord. The family process can sometimes make discussion between reasonable people untenable. And on the societal level, the amount of clashing between Western values and the Islamic world is ever-increasing. The discussion in our communities has become tribal. Unfortunately, modern values have been rooted in the belief that truth is possible and attainable. It is this notion in particular that makes it impossible for people to collaborate around differences of opinion, even within the family.

After doing eight hours of psychotherapy, I would go home and turn on the television news to find that the world appeared to be coming further apart by the day. I the television news intensified the dire nature of the world situation only compounding my despair. "How is it possible that science has become so politicized? How is it possible that facts have no place in contemporary dialogue? How can communities and nations resolve their problems and differences when families can't?"

Today, husbands and wives who once loved each other speak in vile, disparaging terms about their partners. Family members talk about one another as though they live in alternate universes. Each patient tells me their story of pain and estrangement, portraying themselves as victims while being hurtful and critical of others. It is often astonishing how entrenched the stories of family members can be. The anger of a parent toward their child (or vice versa) seems to obscure the good intentions and feelings that each holds for the other. It is discouraging to realize that family members often talk about one another as though they were evil—as though they see each other as living in different worlds.

Before a trip I took to the Middle East to work with Israeli and Palestinian teenagers, I was watching Allen Dershowitz and Paul Zogby—two purportedly thoughtful men—arguing about the conflict in that region. There seemed to be no possibility of bringing clarity or sensibility to the Israeli-Palestinian dilemma. The two men couldn't find common ground. Instead, they each vilified the other's position. Clearly, they were refusing to recognize that they both could be right and that the problem was to find a new, unique perspective. How is it possible for nations and civilizations to come together when thoughtful men won't agree to listen to each other?

This book was originally conceived to help therapists and educators gain a better understanding of evil from a postmodern perspective. These professions in particular—as well as fields such as criminal justice, criminology, law, religion, and philosophy—have long concerned themselves with the origins of poor behavior and wickedness. But as this treatise developed over time, it became clear to me that society as a whole is on the verge of cultural calamity. The rise of either-or thinking, especially fundamentalism, has brought havoc to world order. In places such as Afghanistan, Yemen, Myanmar, and Taiwan, unfolding conflict has become the daily diet. It is horrific to realize that Christians, Muslims, and Jews won't hear out one another's reasonable concerns. How is it that the lessons of the wars in Vietnam and Iraq—or, for that matter, the American Civil War—remain elusive?

It is even more remarkable that people of the same faith despise each other for what they view to be poor practice of their religion. Shiite and Sunni Muslims have been in a deadly struggle over the proper practice of Islam for centuries. In Northern Ireland, Protestants and Catholics have despised and killed one another over disagreements in cultural practices, including the Brexit deal. It is so easy, it seems, to reignite old animosity and hatred.

Back in the United States, fundamentalist Christians shoot and bomb abortion clinics in the name of Christ. Why should this be surprising when religious leaders like Pat Robertson preach that God creates hurricanes to punish sinners who disagree with his beliefs? According to Robertson, this vengeful version of God brings his wrath upon those who believe that a woman has the right to exercise control over her body and have an abortion. So how does Robertson reconcile the death of all the poor storm victims who agree with him? Once again, why can't reasonable people listen to one another?

One of the other purposes of this book is to demonstrate how efforts to find the truth regarding the human condition often lead to unintended outcomes. One such example from psychotherapy is a patient's passivity and dependency on their therapist. Another is the result of some therapists' preoccupation with theory. A therapist's internal dialogue over treatment paradigms often results— unintentionally—in the patient's concerns going unheard. This book will demonstrate how previously held theories and beliefs frequently cause therapists to miss the particular interests of those who approach them for help.

As I hinted at earlier, though, the scope of this book broadened over time to address the need for all of us to reexamine our fundamental belief in the truth—how our internal dialogue and our desire to be correct interfere with our willingness to listen and, ultimately, collaborate with others. As a psychotherapist, I have noticed how people spend little time listening to each other. Before one family member finishes their thoughts, another is formulating their response. Family treatment originally encouraged debate and dialogue during a family session. Today, those of us who participate in postmodern practices ask individuals in the families we work with to sit back and listen to their family's unfolding dialogue, then reflect on the discussion with the treatment team rather than with the family. It appears that much of what is troubling in a family is what is troubling in the world: a reluctance to listen to one another.

This, as a result, becomes the ultimate question: Was culture created to have us believe the unbelievable? Would it be too cynical to think that culture was created to control the masses and subordinate independent thinking? If so, then is it inevitable that as the world shrinks in size, the possibility for cultures to go to war with one another increases? Or is this push toward fundamental thinking the unintended outcome of our ultimate belief in the pursuit of truth?

It is my intention to reflect on those possibilities through this book. It is, of course, possible that both ideas may be at play in today's cultural struggles, just as it is possible that neither explanation will be satisfactory.

Within the general culture as well as psychotherapy literature, there has been a long-standing interest in the discussion of evil and wickedness. Beginning before the modernist concern with abnormality and psychopathology, the problem of poor and unusual behavior was the domain of religion. Despite the extensive discussion of evil and abnormality residing within the organization and development of the self, this book will locate the problem of evil in the social construction of society.

Modern society requires that we accept its truths. Yet, over and over again, our culture and religions ask us to have faith. This book contends that the instinctive forces of curiosity and love challenge society. The emergence of these innate human experiences is problematic to society because they challenge efforts to maintain the continuity—the concept of evil—that has emerged to control our ideas and behavior.

Chapter One: The Problem

The question of poor behavior or wickedness has largely plagued society from its inception. When individuals come together, to form a community a series of rules or conditions are developed to expedite the common good of the group. These laws and regulations are designed to promote the public's "good behavior," but society at times also promoted the concept of evil to establish control beyond the regular functions of law and order.. One only has to look at the struggle created by Putin in the Ukraine. He told the Russian People he had to deal with the Nazifcation of the Ukraine, an obvious lie.

From the onset, Western culture has used the idea of evil spiritual forces or demonic possession to enforce its boundaries. Religion has promulgated fear that not obeying their rules will result in damnation; this was the very idea that was promoted during various Inquisitions. In part, this fear of evil forces has kept communities from straying from traditional boundaries.

Dating back to biblical times, the story of the origins of evil was dominated by demonic spirits. The story of creation was an excellent example. The original text of the Garden of Eden was much thicker than the abridged story of Adam and Eve found in the book of Genesis of the Old Testament. In the original version as found in the Apocrypha, Lilith—not Eve—was Adam's first wife. And depending on a nation's traditions, the story of Lilith takes a slightly different color.

The major narrative was dominated by the idea that Adam desired a love partner. Much like the beast in the Garden of Eden, he wished to engage in sex. Lilith was a woman of great passion, and she also wished to be dominant in her relationship with Adam. In some traditions, Lilith went to God and asked to be the more powerful one. In others, Adam forced Lilith to lie beneath him. In either case, Lilith is offended by God's indifference to her concern and curses out both him and Adam before fleeing the garden. Muslims were so insistent on males having the superior position in relationships that they said, "Accursed be the man who maketh woman heaven and himself earth."[1] Interestingly, Western patriarchs chose to eliminate Lilith from religious tradition. However, she lived on for over a thousand years. Well into the Middle Ages, the Jews were still using amulets to keep away the lilium, Lilith's descendants. These lustful she-demons desired to copulate with men in their dreams, causing nocturnal emissions.[2] Evil could—and would—more easily overwhelm a man when he was sexually excited.

The original discussion of the relationship between men and women provided a more comprehensive evaluation of the nature of sexual politics. Yet most of us never encountered this enriched version of the creation story. Did the authors of the Bible believe that their contemporaries couldn't handle the discussion's complexity? Were they concerned that bringing these ideas to the forefront would encourage women to challenge the developing male patriarchy? Regardless, it was believed that the idea that a man's loss of sensibility was the source of evil. And despite the many influences on culture, evil persisted as a function of internal force on a man's capability to think clearly—in other words, a function of being compromised by one's disturbed thinking or lack of control over internal feeling states.

In his seminal work *Civilization and Its Discontents*, Sigmund Freud recognized that people's instincts were often destructive and at odds with community survival. He supported the idea that it was in the best interest of the individual and society to formulate agreements that reduce the risk of aggression and harm upon others. He did note, however, that this was at the loss of human freedom and creativity.[3]

A problem at the heart of this discussion is that wickedness or evil is understood as residing within the individual. Furthermore, the understanding of the phenomena of evil requires an answer to the question as to how institutions created for doing "good and moral" work become the cause of immoral actions.

As I mentioned in the introduction, this book contends that evil does not reside within an individual. Rather, the circumstances for the development of evil are created by a confluence of beliefs or actions that foster immoral behavior and destruction. The context for evil is enhanced through the convergence of these four factors:

Binary thinking (i.e., "us versus them")

Control of information (e.g., limiting the free exchange of ideas, restricting access to information)

Overly simplistic solutions to complex problems

Power over behavior (e.g., one group using its strength to limit another's freedom or effectiveness)

Evil is a social construct. It is not a truth that exists independently of the ideas and context of the historical events in which it occurs. Postmodernists frequently have been accused of lacking core concepts of ethics to guide them in a discussion of ideas such as evil. This couldn't be further from the truth. Thus, evil and wickedness are being reevaluated within the moral and ethical guidelines postmodern therapists have embraced. As Albert Einstein once said, "Whoever undertakes to set himself up as a judge in the field of Truth and Knowledge is shipwrecked by the laughter of the gods."[4]

The overriding concepts of a postmodern discussion of evil are as follows:

1. Curiosity is the good and natural state of humankind. All learning and mastery are rooted in this instinctual condition of our being.

Previously held beliefs and narratives should be deconstructed. It is important to comprehend the derivation of ideas in the historical context in which the ideas were or are developed.

Ideas are evolutionary, always open to new definitions and possibilities.

Collaboration between people is useful and preferred to any conversation that is limited or dominated by any particular group or ethos. This can lead to a more complete understanding of situations, the development of more complex solutions, and the sharing of information and points of view.

2. An individual can hold several ideas, perspectives, philosophies, or points of view simultaneously.

All discussion and dialogue can—and should—take place in a loving, affirming manner.

The claim that postmodernism lacks values and deconstructs all moral values to meaninglessness—a claim made by Landon Beyer et.al, in 1992[5]—lacks awareness of the emerging reality of the postmodern therapist. Thus, this review of evil and wickedness occurring within the core values listed above is taken for granted in our culture.

Today, therapists who participate in postmodern practices ask those we work with to sit back and listen to the unfolding dialogue in the family. We ask people in the family to react to the unfolding dialogue of other family members. We encourage family members to witness the family discussion and then reflect with the treatment team rather than with the family. It appears that much of what is troubling in the family is what is troubling in the world. There is an inability to sit back and listen before responding. There is just an inability to listen.

It is my contention that, in many ways, modernism and the institutions of modernity have failed us. In our pursuit of knowledge, we have lost sight of the values of dialogue and collaboration. Universities, for example, have become monuments to modernity, overblown structures that have become mostly obsolete. Even the form of a university, dominated by pedantic professors preaching in large lecture halls, is inconsistent with the nature of learning in our contemporary world. At a time when bright people from different perspectives need to collaborate on solutions to problems, the university maintains separate, artificially segregated departments that compete with one another for stature and resources.

French philosopher René Descartes has sent us on a fool's mission, separating mind from body and philosophy from science. Though many forays have indeed been made into rethinking the nature of higher education, the institution of the university is large, cumbersome, and difficult to change. It needs developing centers that allow people to use critical thinking, creativity, and collaboration. Ironically, business schools have developed curricula that are largely centered around problem-solving. Students are presented with issues from the business community, then called upon to collaborate and resolve the problem using previous education and experience.

As someone who works in the mental health field, I find it absurdly difficult to explain the differences between social work, counseling, and psychology. (For that matter, we might as well add psychiatry and nursing to this discussion.) These departments at colleges and universities have duplicated courses and faculty who never talk or acknowledge one another but rather sit side by side in clinics, hospitals, and offices, doing the same procedures. These anachronistic departments are essentially competing with each other for supremacy.

Chapter Two: How Do We Define Evil?

It is not my intention to suggest that evil does not exist. After all, the destruction of the World Trade Center on September 11, 2011, is undisputedly an evil act. Many of the events taking place around us today (e.g., the Israeli and Palestinian debacle) reek of evil, too. Some may argue that simply defining evil as a social construct ducks the responsibility for determining what is moral and ethical conduct. However, as established in chapter one, there are clear and defined guidelines for moral behavior.

Though it is apparent that evil exists within the community—and that people often behave poorly, unjustly, and hurtfully—it is not a function of demonic possession. It may be, in part, a function of a person's natural tendencies for aggression. In other words, we may sometimes lose control of our natural instincts or our tendencies to be curious and loving. But how and why does this happen? What are the conditions that lead to evil behavior?

Most discussions of wickedness and evil struggle with the concept of classifying which individual acts are at odds with social sensibility. In his book *The Social Animal*, psychologist Elliot Aronson defines an individual's propensity for aggression. He notes that aggression is pervasive in the world—so omnipresent, in fact, that we often seem inured to the terrible scenes around us. He also remembers how, during the Vietnam War, he had seen the horror in his son's eyes as the two of them watched televised images of people running, their bodies on fire, after a napalm bombing. Aronson himself, on the other hand, passively sat by, barely noticing the events unfolding before him.[1]

How is it that we rarely react to or notice the presence of evil in our lives? How can we accept the concept of our marines invading Iraq as a matter of the right and just consequences of doing our duty in the world? How do we determine the difference between acts that lead to tens of thousands of deaths and other events like the killing of innocents in the Twin Towers on 9/11?

In 1997, Saul Levine developed one of the many interesting paradigms for defining evil. Like most definitions of this sort, it centers on evil as an act of the individual or state. Levine's definition includes the ideas of intent, planning, harm, magnitude, affect, remorse, and environmental context.[2] Though most scholars may agree with this concept, it ultimately misses the root of evil. How can we, using such a paradigm, distinguish the Catholic Church's malicious planning of the burning of over 100,000 women and children during the Spanish Inquisition from the bombings of hotels in Bali, Indonesia? Isn't the planning of the Joint Chiefs of Staff similar to the planning of Al-Qaeda leadership? Or, for that matter, is the magnitude of the Jewish Holocaust during World War II more evil than the 16th Street Baptist Church bombing in Birmingham, Alabama, which killed innocent Black children during the Civil Rights Movement?

In discussions of evil, it is readily recognized that not all actions that harm others are considered evil.[3] An individual's actions are evaluated by the degree to which they are consistent with society's goals and objectives as well as the individual's capability to understand these norms. An example of how society constructs its evaluation of evildoing can be seen in the understanding of certain acts of war. Though most soldiers in an army are held harmless for their actions during war, exceptions are made for particularly heinous actions or egregious behavior. Take, for example, society's reaction to the Mỹ Lai massacre during the Vietnam War. On March 16, 1968, during a search and destroy mission in a small village in Vietnam, over 300 people—including women and children—were killed. Though neither the infantry soldiers involved in the massacre nor the senior officers responsible for sending them there were held criminally culpable, one junior officer was found guilty: Lieutenant William Calley.

It was determined that neither the circumstances of that day, nor the understanding by any reasonable soldier of their orders, would lead to such a situation. Furthermore, during Lieutenant Calley's court-martial, it was decided that, because of a lack of evidence, no one above him could be prosecuted. No one, however, questioned whether government policies or the massive frustration of the men of Charlie Company were possibly the underlying basis for this circumstance.

The events at Abu Ghraib prison in Iraq had a similar outcome. During the Iraq War, Muslim prisoners were tortured and humiliated by the military police unit overseeing the prison. Though several participants were prosecuted for their "evil doings," those who set the stage for these events went relatively unscathed. It has been well established that a captured prisoner's humiliation is inconsistent with the values of our civilization. However, circumstances have seemingly led to the possibility that under "appropriate conditions," such acts can be condoned by society. George W. Bush and his administration set this idea into motion through public policy and their benign neglect of conditions in and around the prison, which may have allowed for the development of a context that led to the harmful, dehumanizing abuse.

However, after the events at Abu Ghraib were investigated, no one from the government was held accountable. Eventually, the abuse was dismissed as an aberration. Thus, it is apparent that society defines events as evil based on concepts ranging from expeditiousness and self-serving to the maintenance of power structures.

The judgment of an individual's evil acts is relative to society's tolerance and forgiveness at any point in history. An act, even when it is clearly hurtful or dangerous, may not result in a criminal penalty. Society determines that an individual's actions can—and should—be mitigated by the individual's capacity for understanding their actions. As early as 1581, a legal treatise distinguished those who understood the differences between good and evil from those who did not. As reported on an episode of the PBS program *Frontline* in 2005, part of this treatise reads as follows: "If a madman or natural fool, or a lunatic in the time of his lunacy, . . . do (kill a man), this is no felonious act, for they cannot be said to have any understanding or will."[4]

The modern standard for evaluating criminal responsibility for defendants claiming exoneration for their poor behavior was developed in 1843. Following the attempt by Daniel M'Naghten to kill Sir Robert Peel, the Prime Minister of England at the time, a standard was created for judging a client's "insanity." Insanity is a legal determination of an individual's capability to know right from wrong at the time of committing a harmful act. Since the M'Naghten test, it appears that an individual's acts may be considered deranged rather than evil.

Depending upon a culture's mood and inclination, tolerance for insane acts fluctuates between understanding and forgiveness, anger and recrimination. In 1953, twenty-three-year-old Monte Durham, who had been in and out of prison and mental institutions, had his housebreaking conviction overturned by a federal appellate judge on the grounds that he wasn't responsible for his actions. The court ruled that ". . . his unlawful act was the product of mental disease or mental defect."[5] By the 1970s, the Model Penal Code had established a more restrictive definition of insanity. Based on the case of *United States v. Brawner*, 471 F.2d 969 (1972), it was determined that a person couldn't be held responsible for their acts if those acts were a result of a mental disease or defect and if the individual didn't possess "substantial capacity either to appreciate the criminality of his conduct or to conform his conduct to the requirements of the law."[6]

In 1984, John Hinckley Jr., a mentally ill young man, attempted to assassinate President Ronald Reagan. Though he was unsuccessful, he severely wounded the president and his press secretary, James Brady. Despite the clear understanding that Hinckley was unable to control his behavior, the public was incensed. A movement arose to change the law to guilty by reason of insanity. Individuals who were found guilty in this manner were to be treated for their mental illness until such a time that they were deemed well enough to understand the nature of their acts and then be punished through imprisonment. This demonstrates how the standard by which society tolerates a person's seemingly "bad" behavior is evolutionary at best and inconsistent at worst.

Depending on the historical context of the time, acts of similar magnitudes may or may not be harshly judged. Ironically, following the publishing of *Malleus Maleficarum* by Heinrich Kramer in 1484, 100,000 women and children were burned at the stake during the Spanish Inquisition. The crime, as determined by the inquisitors, was "the general vices of infidelity, ambition, and lust."[7] Yet in sixteenth-century England, lunacy was a mitigating factor to crime. It is clear, upon review of the history of societal standards for the attitudes toward evil and wickedness, that there was neither any inherent determination of an evil act nor any clear and consistent consequences for these acts. Furthermore, it seems that the idea of evil existing within a person, or as an independent force upon a person, is of little or no utility.

When reviewing the ideas that shape Western culture, one is struck by the origins of evil being rooted in the concept of disobeying God. However, it is not the simple act of disobedience that is at the heart of the creation of evil. It seems that, ultimately, pure and "good" people are corrupted by their human instinct of curiosity. Intriguingly, one of the most basic forces governing humankind is consistently the source of a person's demise. One's wish to learn and master their environment may be seen as potentially corrupting their nature. The ancient tale of Pandora is an example of how concerned our ancestors were with our inherent curiosity.

In the myth, Zeus presents Pandora (whom he created) with a box, which is to remain closed. He then sends wrapped in a veil of innocence to Earth, where Epimetheus instantly falls in love with Pandora's beauty. However, Epimetheus recognizes that Zeus may be involved somehow. So he takes the box from Pandora and attempts to put it out of her reach, away from temptation. Ultimately, as Zeus predicted, humankind falls victim to its curiosity. Pandora attempts to retrieve the box from a shelf and drops it to the floor. Darkness falls in the room, and all levels of horrible things slither out of the box. Thus, evil, sorrow, and pain are inflicted upon humans. To this day, the Greek gods remind us of the sin of hubris, or pride. The myth of Pandora in particular serves as a warning for us to avoid aspiring to have the knowledge or ability of a god.

Throughout the history of Western culture there has existed a tension between our natural instinct towards curiosity and the apparent cultural mandate not to exceed the limits of the Gods ,or the powers that The poem "Warning to Children" by Robert Graves comes to mind:

. . . Children, leave the string alone!

For who dares undo the parcel

Finds himself at once inside it,

On the island, in the fruit,

Blocks of slate about his head,

Finds himself enclosed by dappled

Green and red, enclosed by yellow

Tawny nets, enclosed by black

And white acres of dominoes,

With the same brown paper parcel

Still untied upon his knee.

And, if he then should dare to think

Of the fewness, muchness, rareness,

Greatness of this endless only

Precious world in which he says

He lives—he then unties the string.[8]

It must be reiterated that, dating back to biblical times, the story of creation has been the single most influential concept for understanding sin in our culture. Original sin—also known as ha chet hakamon, or "sin of first man"—is a function of Adam's inability to control both his curiosity and his love of Eve. In other words, our

25

ancestors viewed the two most basic and pure instincts of humankind as destructive and vilified. Despite God's warnings not to eat the fruit, Adam (as does Pandora in her own story) persists in his disobedience and falls prey to his curiosity. In both cases, the consequences of the individual's actions are grave and then perpetrated on their descendants.

Does this mean that humanity is ethically debilitated and powerless to rehabilitate itself unless rescued by God? What is it about curiosity—and, for that matter, love—that is so frightening to our ancestors? Clearly, evil is born out of curiosity and passion. Thus, it seems that the two instincts that are archetypal in the human condition—curiosity and love—are together the source of concern to those who are the protectors of God. From early in the development of culture and religion, it was believed that these two natural instincts would undermine societal rules and mores.

One of the many times I was contemplating the question of what leads to evil was when I was sitting next to an Israeli business owner on a flight out of Tel Aviv. At one point, the man asked me what I had been doing in his country. I told him I had been there as part of a project to bring Israeli and Palestinian youth together. He smiled (though I sensed that his smile was more of a polite smirk) and told me that was admirable. I responded by saying that he may have seen me and my group on local television news the previous evening, when my associate Debbie Nathan and I had attended a demonstration in Lod.

"Really?" the man said. "Lod is quite dangerous, and I have never been there. Nor will I ever be there."

It is true that Lod, located about fifteen kilometers from Tel Aviv, is one of the poorest communities in Israel. However, the demonstration I had attended was on behalf of the Bedouin community, who had had permission from Israel's beginnings to move about freely and set up encampments under the stars as they had for centuries. In turn, the Bedouins had always supported the Jewish nation. Eventually, the government found that allowing the Bedouins to set up their communities amid Israel's urban areas was interfering with the communities' commerce and well-being. So they rescinded the carte blanche and proposed moving the Bedouins into housing projects in cities such as Lod. On the day of the demonstration I had attended, the Israeli government was planning to bulldoze the tent community.

"As we approached the demonstration made up of Arabs, Palestinians, and Bedouins," I explained to the business owner on the plane, "I heard someone call out, 'It's Dr. Evan! It's Dr. Evan!' It was a young Palestinian counselor I had worked with during a previous trip to Israel. He was there, supporting the Bedouins. He called out to the community in Arabic, 'This is Dr. Evan! He is here from the US.

27

He is our friend. I can't believe it. He really means what he says! He wants to help.' The crowd broke out in cheers, and people rushed me to touch and hug me."

"You are either out of your mind or really lucky," the business owner retorted.

I smiled. "You haven't been to Lod. Have you ever been to the West Bank?"

"No. It is not allowed!"

"Have you ever been to or seen a checkpoint?"

"No. I imagine it to be way too disturbing."

"Yes, it is quite disturbing," I answered, "and you should take an opportunity to experience the situation."

"I'd rather stay in Tel Aviv and not know," the business owner replied.

Afterward, at 30,000 feet in the air, I continued to reflect on this encounter. I asked myself what about this encounter disturbed me most. Where was this man's curiosity or empathy? At what point does this situation approach becoming evil? When do we stop concerning ourselves with the plights and predicaments of others? How does one lose the capacity to love others? When I had first learned of the Israeli government's decision to renege on their promise to allow Bedouins to move about Israel, I had wondered whether this was poor policymaking. To me, it smacked of power over behavior. The Arab community felt it was another example of "us versus them" thinking.

It wasn't until that flight from Tel Aviv, during my discussion with the Israeli business owner, that I realized the situation met all of the criteria for the development of evil. This was more than poor decision-making on the Israeli government's part. This was, once again, a simplistic solution to a complicated problem. It also highlighted the systematic elimination of necessary information for Israeli citizens to participate in successful decision-making. The business owner was an example of someone unwilling to look at the corruptness of his country's behavior—and now certainly his own. In other words, I had been a witness to a man who had become devoid of his essential humanity.

Chapter Three: Binary Thinking

Dating back to antiquity, our culture has been dominated by a discourse of binary thinking, or an "us versus them" mentality. In other words, people sometimes consider themselves better than those who are outside their cultural practices—and even superior to cultures who actively resist their values. Through Jewish, Christian, and Islamic traditions, the idea of one's kin being superior to another's had been well established. The story of Abraham, the father of all major Western religions, took place nearly 1,700 years before the modem era. By the time the rules of Moses were codified in the Book of Deuteronomy about 1,000 years later, those who didn't follow the rules of tradition were considered to be part of the unclean nations, or ha goyim. It seems that not only were ancient Jews concerned about maintaining the purity of their culture, but also the dominant trend throughout developing societies of the time was the concern of spreading their cultural imperative. From the Hellenic culture of the Greeks to the Persian religion of Zoroastrianism, there was little tolerance for the ideas or beliefs of the other.

Within the Greek tradition, there were different levels of participation. Nearly a third of the population of the city-states of ancient Greece were slaves. While citizens were entitled to the full protection of the law, slaves had no power or status. They had no right to have a family or own property, as well as no political or legal rights.

Sadly, there is no evidence that there were no advocates for the rights of slaves in ancient Greece. Even the great philosopher Aristotle referred to slaves as "living tools." In his work on politics And so the Greeks spread their culture throughout their empire, taking slaves back to their homeland to be laborers.

It is little wonder, then, that the devaluing of others' beliefs can come so easily to world leaders. The basis for such thinking is thousands of years old.

Around the time that the Greeks were expanding their empire, the Persians were developing their monotheistic religion, known as Zoroastrianism. Within this tradition, Zoroaster, the prophet of God ,the lord of light, had a counterpart, the Lord of Darkness, who had a supporting cast of demons and evil spirits. The forces of light and dark were constantly battling against each other, forever bifurcating the world into the forces of good and evil. After the Jews met the Babylonians and learned about Zoroastrianism, the idea of Satan was introduced into Judeo-Christian theology. The story of Isaiah is where the influence of the Persians' religion makes its way into the Bible:

How are you fallen from heaven, day star, son of the dawn! How are you fallen to earth, conqueror of the nations! You said in your heart, "I will ascend to heaven, above the stars of God: I will set my throne on high . . . I will ascend upon the high clouds. . . ." But you are brought down to darkness, to the depths of the pit. (Isa. 14:12-15)

Events on the magnitude of the destruction of the World Trade Center on 9/11 seem possible only when we recognize the impact of "us versus them" thinking on the evolution of religious beliefs. Through the totalizing dialogues of primarily fundamentalist religious practices, people come to believe that one's beliefs and practices of the worship of God are superior to those of another.

In his book *Occidental Mythology*, Joseph Campbell points out that the ancient legend of Darius, the great King of Persia, centered its discourse on the idea that all that was moral and right derived from Darius and his beliefs. Every enemy of the king was an enemy of God and an agent of the "demon of the lie."[2] Why, then, would we be surprised that educated men who have enough technical understanding to fly superjets into the World Trade Center to bring those massive structures to the ground would do such a heinous act? How can men who have lived among us for years commit such harm and violence to our people? It seems that they must perceive us as being other. We, who believe ourselves to be just and good, are understood by these men to be agents of the "demon of the lie."

Of course, the events of 9/11 must be considered evil acts. They are on the magnitude of the evil acts committed by other zealous fanatics against those they perceived as inferior to them. Hitler's actions against humanity (especially the Jewish community), the deeds of the Khmer Rouge against Cambodians, or the horrors inflicted by the Catholic Church against all nonbelievers during the Spanish Inquisition all required their perpetrator's devaluation of other communities as nonhuman.

Recently, I was talking with young marines who had returned from the Iraq War. I asked them what it had been like to have to kill other people. At first, their responses astonished me. Their consensus was that they hadn't killed people—they had killed terrorists. Of course, the marines had to rationalize the killings of others by dehumanizing those they had killed. They needed to view those individuals as "other." Similarly, during the Vietnam War, recruits learned from the time they arrived on base that the enemy was referred to as "Gooks" or other names that are now considered offensive. In such instances, the military makes every effort to present the enemy as akin to the agents of Satan.

Even in the criminal justice system, it is apparent that those who inflict hurt upon others frequently think in a binary manner. One such example is John Salvi, a man from Brookline, Massachusetts, who demonized those who worked within Planned Parenthood enough that he attacked two abortion clinics on December 30, 1994. His lawyer argued that Salvi was insane at the time of the killings. However, Salvi was found guilty of murder for his actions.

Regardless of whether Salvi was insane, his thinking was binary. He, along with those who have celebrated his actions, considered the staff and doctors performing their duties at abortion clinics to be evildoers. At one point during his trial, he called out, "This is what you get. You should pray the rosary."[3] Irrespective of traditional forensic concerns regarding the evaluation of insanity, individuals who do evil acts frequently dichotomize the world into an "us versus them" division. Ironically, these individuals also believe they are doing the work of God.

David Berkowitz, also known as the Son of Sam, is another infamous killer, terrorizing New York City in 1977. Initially, Berkowitz was determined to be insane. However, just as in the Salvi case, Berkowitz perceived the world in a binary manner. In a letter to Captain Joseph Borrelli of the New York City Police Department, he wrote [with misspellings intact], "I feel like an outsider. I am on a different wave length than everybody else—programmed too kill."[4] Thus, it appears that whether an individual is determined to be sane or insane, the act of evil requires perpetrators to distance themselves from those they inflict harm upon. Much like Salvi, Berkowitz— though he admitted to knowing he was a monster—believed he was authorized by a higher power to "'[g]o out and kill' commands father Sam."[5]

If binary thinking is one of the characteristics of the construction of evil, then what of situations like psychotherapy or education? Does binary thinking poorly affect the results of "treatment" or "pedagogy"? Is it possible that the dominant discourse between doctor and patient or teacher and student portends possible unintended destructive consequences on the outcomes of these endeavors? As noted by philosophers such as Michel Foucault, many of the ideas we take for granted in society today have origins that are surprisingly disconnected from their purpose or usage.[6] One might even conclude that the medical model in psychotherapy was a quirk of history rather than an intended outcome.

As Foucault noted, the origins of the contemporary psychiatric hospital date back to the General Hospital of Paris around 1650. During the seventeenth century, Europe was undergoing a great deal of change. Peasants were moving from the countryside to the newly developing cities. These people needed care and assistance, and they struggled to find employment in the new mercantile economy. Hospitals began as centers to collect the homeless and indigent and get them off the streets. In England, these institutions were referred to as poorhouses. From there, medicine and psychiatry developed in hospitals as humane efforts to deal with the downtrodden citizens' challenges. Between 1750 and 1850, much effort was made to classify and understand the nature of individuals who were distressed by their life circumstances, and the medical model requiring a sick patient and an expert physician came into being.[7]

The medical model in psychotherapy is structured in a binary manner. It assumes that, much like in a doctor-patient situation in physical medicine, a patient approaches a therapist for relief from internal dysfunction and breakdown and possibly external demands or stress. In either case, the patient does not have the resources or capability to find relief without the support of or intervention by an expert. Although this model has often been useful to assist individuals who are struggling with life problems and stressors, the unintended outcome may have intensified self-doubt and shame for patients. If the intended outcome of psychotherapy is to assist individuals in being independent or self-reliant, then the idea of psychotherapy based on binary thinking—an expert doctor bringing relief to a despairing patient—may be counterproductive.

Unfortunately, psychotherapy frequently leads to a patient's dependency on the psychotherapist. This reinforces the individual's lack of belief in their internal resources. Thus, the binary logic of the medical model may ultimately make that model destructive to personal integrity and well-being.

Similarly, the role of binary thinking in education may interfere with the goals of the educational process. All too often in the contemporary classroom, the student is the passive recipient of information from their "expert teachers." For millennia, society has celebrated the Socratic method of dialogic teaching. Yet despite centuries of data suggesting that education requires the development of creative, involved thinkers, we have abandoned educational models that require collaborative learning for models that teach facts to help students pass exit exams.

It is apparent that the education of those behind the 9/11 terrorist attacks was steeped in binary thinking. Islamic fundamentalist schools heavily indoctrinate their pupils with an "us versus them" mentality. The structure of these schools is one where the powerful mullah presents his ideas, beliefs, and philosophies to his passive recipients. This information is often biased and limited (which we will discuss further in chapter four). It is little wonder, then, that we have confronted instances like when Maria Ressa, former CNN bureau chief in Jakarta, Indonesia, reported on February 26, 2004, that the saying "Death in the way of Allah is our highest aspiration" was hanging from the ceiling of a classroom in the Islamic school she was visiting.[8]

It is easy to understand that the roots of evil are sown in environments that devalue other cultures and societies. However, is it possible for education to become the scaffolding for the development of individuals who passively receive such ideas? Fundamentalists within American society have made it known that they prefer schools to teach their values and philosophy to all students regardless of their culture. The teaching of creationism in the science classroom is one of their attempts to indoctrinate all children with their belief system.

However, the problem of binary thinking is—and can be—much subtler than one group's attempts to assert their values over another. During a discussion I had with graduate students in my course on abnormality, I asked the class whether they believed in Darwin's evolutionary theory. One student responded, " of course not "God created the world in six days and rested on the seventh." I was astonished and responded " How do you account for dinosaur bones found in the earth." The student responded a trick played by the devil. I asked the class how many of them agreed with the student, a third of the twenty four students supported their class mate.

Becoming interested in the ideas that often went untalked about in class but were the scaffolds of my students thinking, I then asked the class how many of them believed America was the most successful country on Earth, The majority of students reported that America was the freest society in the world. But when I asked those students if they had researched this idea, none of them said they had. One student responded, "Everyone knows that we are the greatest country in the world, with the best standard of living." The rest of the class concurred with this assumption.

I pressed my students further, asking them questions such as "How does our society compare to that of the Netherlands?" and

"How do Europeans view their lifestyle in comparison to ours?" I wanted to know where these beliefs originated from. Was it possible—and is it still possible—that the passive acceptance of aphorisms such as "America is the greatest country on Earth" is rooted in the classroom's binary structure? Have we considered that the cultural and historical drift, dating back to antiquity, has led us to structural forms in the community that prepare us for accepting binary thinking?

One of my experiences that illustrates how we deal with the other in society occurred when I was training Palestinian counselors in Beit Jala, a small town near Bethlehem on the West Bank. The participants had had a difficult trek to get to the training, coming from places like Ramallah, Nablus, and Tulkarm. These communities were only an hour or so away from the training site as the crow flies. But because of checkpoints and regulations, the trip took up to a day for some folks.

After the first morning of the training, most of the participants joined me for lunch in the dining hall. Debbie, my co-leader and the founder of Artsbridge, was dealing with the many complications of running a program in Israel, so she wasn't present. As I sat with the Palestinian counselors—some of whom were Muslim, others Christian—one woman from Tulkarm asked if she could confide in me. I said yes.

39

"Well," the woman from Tulkarm continued, "most of us here really like you and value your participation. But we neither trust nor like Debbie."

"Why is that?" I asked.

"Because she is a Jew!"

"You traveled so far to come here. Why would you do that?"

"Well even if she is a Jew, she at least shows interest in our plight. You, however, appear to be a kind and informed leader."

"What if I were to tell you I am also a Jew?"

The woman from Tulkarm seemed bewildered. "That's not possible. I genuinely like you!"

"If that's the case, this journey was well worth it for me," I retorted.

How much of our thought processes or the ideas we hold to be true reflect the structural dynamic by which we learn? Almost twenty-five years ago, I conducted a research project on the mechanisms children use to develop their lens for understanding the world. At the time, my colleagues and I developed a method of scoring family styles and structure that was similar to scoring responses to Rorschach cards. I would give a series of scores to a family throughout a session while one of my associates would independently score their identified child patient on actual Rorschach cards. The correlation between the scores on family dynamics and the scores of the single child's understanding of the ambiguous cards was extremely high. To this day, it is unclear how to explain these results. Suffice it to say, something about the stories, structure, and style of the family is internalized by the child, becoming their basis for interpreting the world.

Does the classroom's binary style become incorporated in this manner as a lens for interpreting future knowledge? Are we then responsible for carefully understanding the consequences of this style of education? Should we be concerned that a possible unintended consequence of the student-teacher dichotomy is the establishment of roots of evil? Whatever the causes for binary thinking, may be such attitudes have become deeply rooted in our culture. We must ask why it is so difficult for individuals to leave a specific religion or political party for another.

The reality is, we have become a tribal culture. We need only look to the United States Congress to see how the country has become binary in its functions. After the insurrection at the United States Capitol on January 6, 2021, one could have assumed that Americans would come together on their attitudes toward the nature of the events. However, neither the general public nor their representatives in Congress did so, and the country remained split by a ratio of almost two to one. Yet, even though we all witnessed the insurrection on television, Republican representatives claimed that the events were similar to other peaceful demonstrations. Andrew S. Clyde, a Republican representative from Georgia, even downplayed the events as "acts of vandalism" and suggested it was a "boldfaced lie" to call what happened that day an insurrection.[9] Meanwhile, Alexandria Ocasio-Cortez, a Democratic representative from New York, said, "We are not safe with people who hold positions of power who are willing to endanger the lives of others if they think it will score them a political point."[10]

Chapter Four: The Limiting of Information

It is understood in modern society that information is power. Thus, individuals who have access to information about technology, economics, or even politics have power over those who are less informed. This is not a new phenomenon. People who have controlled the development of science and technology have also controlled the direction and outcomes of world history. Before the modern era—or about 42,000 years ago—the inventors of sea travel began inhabiting the far reaches of the world. And approximately 11,000 years before Christ was born, those who created the necessary tools for planting grain also developed the first communities and, ultimately, the rules by which society would operate. Finally, the Sumerians of Mesopotamia—the people of the first great civilization, living between the Tigris and Euphrates rivers—invented the wheel, allowing them to develop agriculture, transportation, and warfare almost 6,800 years before the Common Era.

Today, nations compete with one another for technological supremacy in communications, energy, transportation, and economics. One such example is the recent conflict developing between China and the United States, as both countries attempt to control the flow of information and ideas through the Internet.

For our purposes in discussing the origins of evil, suffice it to say that we quickly understood that those who controlled knowledge and information would have the power to control others. As noted in chapter one those who codified the Old Testament of the Bible abridged the thicker, more complex narratives of their times to expedite the development of the rules they wished to introduce to the culture. Stories that were not included in the Bible are known as the Apocrypha. In Greek, the word *apocrypha* literally means "hidden text." As Sophocles once said, "I have attempted to tear asunder the veil you have hung to conceal from us the pain of life, and I have been wounded by the mystery[1]. It seems that, dating back to the ancient Greeks, intelligent men wished to understand the complex mysteries of life. However, Sophocles reminds us that the gods punished mortals for the sin of hubris. Thus, the truth may blind us. Who are we to presume that we can know or act like a god? How do we understand this tension between our curious nature and the prohibition of our culture toward "knowing"?

Likewise, evidence suggests that our ancestors were unwilling to tolerate challenges to their authority—challenges that were inevitable once people had access to unabridged information. Over and over again, we have been told that knowing too much can and would be disastrous to our well-being. So how can we possibly accept the

Warren Commission's report on President John F. Kennedy's assassination? The details of this report were suppressed for twenty-five years because it seemed the common people can't be trusted to know how to react or interpret these facts. More recently, George W. Bush and his administration presented data to the world to substantiate their reasons for invading Iraq. They introduced the idea of weapons of mass destruction to mobilize support for their previously developed intentions. Despite much data that questioned this position, the Bush administration chose only to share the "facts" that supported their choice.

Inevitably, the suppression of information can lead to mischief and wrongdoing. During the seventeenth century, the Catholic Church chose to hide and ultimately repudiate the advances taking place in science. At one point, Nicolaus Copernicus, through mathematical calculations, had proposed that the Earth, as well as the other planets, revolved around the Sun. Later, Galileo Galilei, a professor at the University of Padua, concluded through mathematics and the use of the newly developed telescope that Copernicus's calculations were correct. A devout Catholic, Galileo had never considered that his conclusions would bring him in conflict with Church authorities. Unfortunately, Cardinal Robert Bellarmine, acting on directions from the Roman Inquisition, disagreed with Galileo. The inquisitors found that these new ideas were in direct opposition to the Scriptures. The Church held that Psalms 93 and 104, as well as Ecclesiastes 1:5, spoke of the motion of celestial bodies and the suspended position of the Earth.

Galileo never intended to disparage the Catholic Church when he took Saint Augustine of Hippo's position on the Scriptures—that was, not to take every passage literally. However, he was determined to move knowledge forward. In 1633, he wrote, "I do not feel obliged to believe that the same god who has endowed us with sense, reason, and intellect has intended us to forgo their use."[2] In reality, the Church knew that Galileo was correct. But by questioning their position, he embarrassed them. The Church was also fearful that the reversal of their long-held position on geocentrism would disillusion the masses.

Tragically, Galileo was convicted by the Roman Inquisition for heresy. His books were banned from sale in Rome, and he was confined to his home under house arrest until his death in 1642.

Over 1,000 years before the Roman Inquisition unjustly punished Galileo, the Catholic Church was concerned with limiting ideas that challenged their interpretation of the Gospels. In her book *The Gnostic Gospels*, Elaine Pagels, a professor of theology at Princeton University, describes the extremes taken by the Church to eliminate thinking that undermined their power and authority. For instance, in Nag Hammadi, Egypt, a series of manuscripts were unearthed in 1955 that questioned some of the basic tenets of Christianity. Despite the interesting and sometimes divergent thinking presented in these volumes, the general public is still largely unaware of their existence. Though no direct evidence was found, knowledge of these books had existed for some time. One possible example is *Against Heresies: On the Detection & Overthrow of the So-Called Gnosis*, a five-volume treatise written by the bishop Irenaeus of Lyons around AD 180 that condemned as heretics certain Christians who professed the blasphemous ideas of the Gnostics.[3]

There were originally fifty-two volumes found at Nag Hammadi. Unfortunately, some of these volumes were destroyed by those who found them. Included in the volumes that remained were the Gospel of Thomas, the Gospel of Mary (Magdalene), and the Gospel of Philip. If you are familiar with the Gospels, you may notice the differences in this excerpt from the original Gospel of Philip found in the New Testament:

The companion of the [Savior is] Mary Magdalene. [But Christ loved] her more than [all] the disciples, and used to kiss her [often] on her [mouth]. The rest of [the disciples were offended]. . . . They said to him, "Why do you love her more than all of us?" The Savior answered and said to them, "Why do I not love you as (I love) her?"[4]

The implication of this passage is obvious. It is little wonder, then, that the founders of the Catholic Church wished to suppress the volumes that were eventually discovered at Nag Hammadi. Thomas and Mary Magdalene were contemporaries of Jesus. Their gospels to his words and deeds, though similar to those codified in the New Testament, make Jesus accessible to each of us without the need for a Church hierarchy. Furthermore, the passage puts women on par with men. It leaves open the possibility of female divinity.

In a similar example dating back to AD 400, after Constantine adopted Christianity as the religion of the Romans, priests had the power to command the police. Following the Council of Nicea, the priests ordered all Gospels that were not considered part of the Church doctrine to be destroyed. Thus, all followers of the Gnostic Gospels were deemed heretics and banished from Rome.

Thomas, in his Gospel, tells us that Jesus came to bring enlightenment to man. Instead of coming to save us from sin, he came to guide us to spiritual understanding. In the same version of this Gospel, Jesus says, "I am not your master. Because you have drunk, you have become drunk from the bubbling stream which I have measured out. . . . He who will drink from my mouth will become as I am: I myself shall become he, and the things that are hidden will be revealed." [5] The Jesus of the Gnostic tradition wasn't binary in his thinking. His concepts were not rooted in an "us versus them" mentality, nor were they static truths. This Jesus was dialogic, collaborative, and evolutionary, allowing truth to emerge from self-exploration.

Galileo was offended by a philosophy that claimed the Bible was a literal statement. He believed in a God that gave people the capacity to reason and think. He used Saint Augustine as a model of higher-level thinking. Augustine himself had had difficulty with individuals who tried to make deductions about the world through a literal translation of Genesis. He expands on this concern in this excerpt from *The Literal Meaning of Genesis*, as translated by John H. Taylor:

Usually, even a non-Christian knows something about the earth, the heavens, and other elements of the world, about the motion and orbit of the stars and even their size and relative positions, about the predictable eclipses of the sun and the moon, the cycles of the year. . . . Reckless and incompetent expounders of the Holy Scripture bring untold sorrow on the wiser brethren when they are caught in one of their mischievous and false opinions and are taken to task by those who are by the authority of our sacred books.[6]

Today, there are still those who would have us believe that they are "knowers of truth and knowledge," those who wish to put an end to the long history of questioning in our culture. Fundamentalists who are currently in power prefer that we interpret the Bible literally and live by the rules that they believe to be true. They would eliminate one's right to privacy or a woman's right to control her body, or tell us that homosexuality is a disease. All of these ideas are supposedly substantiated by their understanding of the Scriptures.

Similarly, Constitutionalists often don't understand that the Constitution of the United States is a living, breathing document. The authors of the Constitution couldn't have possibly envisioned all of the changes that society would endure after the document was written. Rather, they gave Americans a framework from which we could find our way to solving the dilemmas of our time. If those in power today had their way, even legal precedents that saved us from the continuation of segregation (think *Brown v. Board of Education*) would be in question. The internment of Japanese Americans by the US government during World War II—now considered an evil act—would be considered correct. Interestingly, the Jesus portrayed in the Gnostic Gospel of Thomas said, "And he said, 'Whoever finds the interpretation of these sayings will not experience death.'"[7] These ancient words encourage us to look for answers within ourselves and not accept the rules and explanations of our high priests. Unfortunately, the same high priests chose to exclude those words from the Bible.

The limiting of information at the societal level is the background for understanding how this lack of can be considered acceptable at microlevels of communication. When one observes the context in which psychotherapy and psychodiagnosis take place, it is apparent that limited perspective and limited information can cause major consequences in people's lives. It is common practice to label identified patients (IPs)—particularly identified children—based on the testimony of others. Teachers and parents often determine a child's wellness independent of the context from which it comes. Though it is clear to myself and others who practice family therapy that an IP's behavior is often reactive to or a part of the family system or even society, it is still common to send the individual for treatment as though only that individual was the problem. My psychotherapy practice has often included children who are considered treatment-resistant. These children carry several diagnoses and are often medicated. The idea that these identified children are not the problem rarely occurs to their clinicians. Modern clinical assumptions are rooted in the belief that the previous identification and location of a problem within a patient is based on objective reality and is valid.

I was once asked to be a consultant for a case where an eleven-year-old boy hadn't made significant improvement after five years of psychodynamically oriented psychotherapy; He was diagnosed with bipolar disorder, attention deficit disorder with hyperactivity, and oppositional defiant disorder. At the time of the consultation, the major concern to the boy's mother and his therapist was his angry outbursts at his younger sister, who was seven. The boy was attending weekly therapy sessions and had been having monthly collateral sessions with his mom. He was taking antidepressants, a mood stabilizer, and stimulants. The younger sister was described as having "some learning difficulties" but wasn't a participant in the treatment. The consultation was done as a family meeting with a reflecting team.

The identified child—in other words, the boy—was placed on the reflecting team while the mother and sister were interviewed by the child's therapist. Ironically, after one consultation, many of the issues and problems of the boy "dissolved," a term used by Harlene Anderson and Harold A. Goolishian in their research for *Family Process*.[8]

How could this have happened? From a collaborative language perspective, significant information that had never been known before was obtained during one family interview, and significant change occurred as a result.

The first difficulty was the misidentification of the problem. The child wasn't responding to treatment because he wasn't the problem. As long as the clinicians persisted in treating a child who—though possibly symptomatic—wasn't ultimately the issue, the situation couldn't improve. The information that was necessary to successfully identify and treat the problem had been overlooked for five years.

The acceptance of a parent's testimony (i.e., the authorization of the narrative of the "patient's problem" by a limited source) often proves to be distracting or unhelpful. As with the larger cultural imperatives requiring more data and insight than the authorities are ready or willing to reveal, the family can't move to a new, more satisfying organization. Kenneth Gergen and John Kaye refer to the phenomena of professionals accepting the presentation of a client as the "advisory option."[9] Until there appears to be utility or viability to this option, no real progress can ensue.

The second problem was that the professionals and the mother were not listening to the identified child's concerns or narratives. Unfortunately, the ideas introduced by the mother subordinated the child's perspective. Again, Gergen and Kaye have posited that seeing a situation through the single lens of a particular theory or paradigm precludes the opportunity to see all the possibilities for understanding and resolving a problem.[10] Similarly, seeing the problem from one individual's perspective prevents a wider understanding of the issues. Just as it is biased and limited to try to understand the Israeli-Palestinian conflict through only one lens, trying to understand family problems through limited input leads to limited possibilities. By putting the child on the reflecting team, we allowed the child to listen to the family dilemma more clearly and the mother and clinicians hear him more clearly. Thus, the therapists, the family, and the reflecting team provided alternative possibilities for establishing meaning and understanding in the family.

The third problem concerns the nature of meaning-making and the family epistemology. Just as in the macro issues of society, certain ideas are taken for granted. We may assume that all the members of one family make sense of ideas and issues using the same internal taxonomy. Yet different family members frequently find different meanings for the same language. As Anderson points out, it is imperative that therapists—or, for that matter, all of us—carefully understand the meaning of words and metaphors to each individual: Thus, the correspondents must explore the use of specific language to that individual. Similarly, therapists must attempt to join their clients in the client's system of meaning-making.[11]

This does not mean that it is evil to misunderstand the language of clients. However, the consequences of a therapist assuming that they understand a clinical situation can create great misery for their patients. In the clinical case where I was hired as a consultant, the boy was put through unnecessary ardor because of the mental health system's intractability. During those five years, no one apparently thought to reassess the nature and development of the stated problem. The boy eventually internalized the mythology that developed around his dysfunction, and he accepted ideas such as "I can't control my anger."

Ironically, during this interview, the boy sat quietly for approximately twenty minutes while watching his sister fail to control herself, After a more careful discussion with the boy, it became clear that his sister's difficulties were being ignored by their mother—and, for that matter, had gone unnoticed by the clinicians. The adults' expectations for the boy to care for his younger sister and control his feelings often led him to being overwhelmed. Though he would corroborate the assessment of his mother to his therapist, the meaning of this statement was unlike the ideas clinicians often have around anger management. More precisely, the boy's idea was a complicated statement: "I can't do what my mother expects of me. I can't tell her of my discomfort, and I become overwhelmed."

The concepts about language acquisition and development are essential for the boy's therapists to comprehend the complex development of his thoughts. The philosopher who provided the rationale for Galileo's challenge of the Catholic Church also shaped the discussion of language acquisition for many centuries. Saint Augustine understood language as the learning of symbols or names for objects, as he wrote in *The Confessions*: "When they (my elders) named some object, and accordingly moved toward something, I saw this and I grasped that the thing was called by the name they uttered."[12] In other words, if a parent holds up a shiny red fruit and names it an apple, this will be the child's symbol for this object.

More recently, philosopher Ludwig Wittgenstein demonstrated that the rules of language development are far more complex and that other factors are involved in the development of ideas: "A main source of our failure to understand is that we do not command a clear view of the use of our words."[13] This shows that Wittgenstein understood how the set of rules or logic below the surface of the words one uses help exemplify the meaning of a statement.

Therapists frequently assume that when a child says they are having difficulty containing their anger, it means that the child "lacks control." In the instance with the boy whose case I was consulting, it meant many things including, "I don't have the power to stand up to my mother." Wittgenstein suggests in his writings that the simple naming of objects is only a portion of language development. Language acquisition and development requires learning the rules of a word game that give meaning to the words, thoughts, and ideas. It is imperative to learn the meaning or the "rules" behind the meaning in a given family context—or, for that matter, a given society. Just as Wittgenstein argues that not only does the naming of an object give it meaning but that also the use of the word signifies its meaning, the family rules—both spoken and unspoken—modify the meaning of ideas expressed by family members.

Much evil has occurred because individuals didn't understand or chose to manipulate others through the use of language. Clearly, we all understand calling out "Fire!" in a crowded hall can lead to panic. But what are the consequences of teaching people that those who believe in a woman's right to choose are sinners? Might that lead to the bombing of abortion clinics or the shooting of doctors? And what are the consequences of parents telling therapists that their children can't control their anger? Might that lead to years of unnecessary therapy and the label of being mentally ill?

Ironically, during the twenty-first century—an age of technological achievement and information proliferation—large portions of the population seem unable to accept the truth when they hear it. Even more of a paradox is the fact that the distrust of governments and institutions has led to the rejection of scientific development and the proclamations of concern by the government.

Donald Trump has mastered the art of distorting information and tapping into the fears of many. In May 2019, Sean Illing of the American Press Institute pointed out that then-President Trump had mastered the news cycle by collaborating with Fox News to tilt journalism toward his own goals.[14] Yet Trump has done much more than alter the news cycle to meet his goals. As Thomas B. Edsall wrote in December 2016, "[T]he continuous alteration of the past and in the long run probably demands a disbelief in the very existence of objective truth."[15]

In an episode of *The Diane Rehm Show* that aired on November 30, 2019 Scottie Nell Hughes, a Trump supporter, said, "There's no such thing anymore as facts. And so Mr. Trump's tweets among a certain crowd—a large part of the population—are truth."[16] By saying this, Hughes means that we are in the age of doublespeak. Trump and his allies, along with a large portion of the US population, are in a perpetual echo chamber. For instance, Trump said in one of his tweets that he has facts that the 2020 election was stolen, and his supporters respond by saying that our government must be saved from those who are corrupting our democracy. In turn, Trump and his Republican allies reply by saying that we must support the large portion of the population who believe the election was stolen. Of course, there is no evidence that the election was stolen—only the tweets of a maniacal, self-serving president.

On March 23, 2021, NBC News reported that former Trump attorney Sidney Powell's campaign to invalidate the 2020 election wasn't based on fact. Her lawyers stated, "No reasonable person would conclude that the statements were truly statements of fact." Powell and Rudy Giuliani, both of whom were a part of Trump's legal team, had argued that there was a conspiracy to overthrow the election. Among other issues, they said that the conspiracy included Dominion machines and deceased dictator Hugo Chávez of Venezuela. "The conspiracy involved all kinds of interests of globalists," Powell said. "Dictators, corporations—you name it. Everybody's against us except President Trump." Powell's lawyers went on to say that her statements were so outrageous, they were unbelievable.[17] No reasonable person would listen to Trump's lawyers. However, much of the population did listen—and they are still trying to overthrow the most successful election in US history.

Chapter Five: Simple Solutions to Complex Problems

Throughout history, there have been countless attempts to solve society's complex problems with overly simplistic solutions. Binary thinking and a lack of information seem to further reinforce a person's propensity to think in limited, stereotypical ways. The archetypal fable of "The Three Little Pigs" is one such example that has taken many forms over time, including the version found in *Grimms' Fairy Tales*. The gist of this tale is that the careful, diligent third little pig builds a house of stone to protect him and the other pigs from the Big Bad Wolf—but not before the rushed, thoughtless behavior of the first two pigs jeopardizes their survival.

Though we must be thoughtful and diligent in our efforts, history has been littered with the thoughtless, simplistic answers of our leaders. Despite cultural imperatives such as Samuel Johnson's "He that never thinks can never be wise" or Confucius's "A man who does not think and plan long ahead will find trouble right at his door," there are endless examples of mindless, morally bankrupt, and unsuccessful attempts to confront societal challenges. Open the newspaper on any given day, and you can find instances of how contemporary culture avoids confronting difficult realities. We need not look any further than the issue of climate change to see how reluctant our government is to face that massive challenge. And if you look back over the first decade of the twenty-first century, you will find two particular news items that have blatantly demonstrated these phenomena: comments made by James Hansen, former chief meteorologist at NASA, about the George W. Bush administration's suppression of information about climate change; and the handling of the image of Muhammad by European newspapers.

Let's look first at Hansen's example, since that may be the more obvious of the two IN 2008], Hansen told the press that he was being "handcuffed" by the Bush administration against revealing his concerns about global warming. He believed that, at the current rate of greenhouse gas emissions, the Earth's temperature would rise by five degrees in the next hundred years to a benchmark not seen in the past three million years. He went on to say, "[That] would bring the seas to a time when they were eighteen stories higher than they are today."[1]

Throughout his presidency, George W. Bush had told the world that there was no sufficient data to suggest that pollutants were affecting global warming. According to him, there was no scientific evidence of the greenhouse effect. Since then, the public has learned (thanks to Hansen and others) that not only had Bush misunderstood the impact of his ignorance and poor decision-making on the world's condition, but he was also suppressing the necessary data for the successful amelioration of this problem.

This highlights a whole other problem that occurs when those in power don't have the information—or, worse, the capability—to make good decisions regarding potentially calamitous events. However, ignoring and suppressing the information that is necessary to stave off catastrophe borders on evildoing. How do we explain to the future residents of New Orleans—or New York City, Miami, Los Angeles, and all the world's coastlines—that George W. Bush was responsible for suppressing the necessary data to save them? Will we think of Bush as an evil person in the future? Even a decade after his presidency, we still haven't responded sufficiently to the dangers of climate change.

Fast-forward to the late 2010s and early 2020s. Hundreds of thousands of acres of forests burned up in the western United States as well as the Australian outback. Towns and cities in Europe were inundated by floods. Storm after storm overwhelmed the states of the Gulf Coast. What level of calamity needs to occur before we stop fighting with each other and find solutions to these complex events? What prevents large segments of our population from reacting to the danger before them?

The second news item I referred to earlier came from the Danish newspaper *Jyllands-Posten* in 2005. That year, the paper ran twelve cartoons depicting Muhammad, and among these renderings was one of the prophets wearing a turban made of a nuclear bomb. The newspaper had searched for a rendering of Muhammad that they ultimately couldn't find and subsequently learned from a publisher of children's books that the image of Muhammad was impossible to find because it is prohibited within Islamic culture to create a likeness of him.

The problem here is the poor, simplistic ways in which all parties dealt with the dilemma. The Islamic population of European countries was initially incensed by the paper's insensitivity toward Islamic culture. They called for the punishment of those responsible for the insult. *Jyllands-Posten*, though apologizing for their indiscretion, noted that in the "free world," freedom of the press exists. Matters were further confounded when other European newspapers, in the spirit of the "free press," chose to support their colleagues in Denmark by reprinting the original, hurtful cartoons in their papers. A more thoughtful, careful solution to this dilemma would have likely reduced the disastrous consequences in Europe and the Middle East.

Each side continued to respond in an overly simplistic fashion, bringing continued hurt and hardship to the region. First, though the newspapers had the so-called right to exercise free speech, they also had the right to use restraint. *Jyllands-Posten* could have done more than apologize for their indiscretion. Instead, they could have opened the paper to a series of articles by leading Islam scholars and clerics that would have explained their religion and culture to Christian Europe. Likewise, the free media of Europe could have joined with *Jyllands-Posten* in celebrating Europe's diversity.

Obviously, the Islamic world has been incensed with the United States and Europe. It has responded to centuries of being devalued with venomous anger. Western civilization has depicted the Islamic world as "out-of-control zealots."The world witnessed the consequences of "us versus them" thinking. However, the continued violent outbursts within the Islamic world bring us closer to a catastrophic clash between cultures and reinforces current Western stereotypes. Leaders within Islam could have called for restraint while pointing out the continued ignorance of American and European cultures. Islamic newspapers could have promoted an exchange of ideas with their European counterparts. More thoughtful and complex solutions would have called for an exchange of the peoples of both cultures. Peoples from all walks of life,.and the younger the children who participate in these exchanges, the greater the opportunity for developing familiarity between people.

As noted in chapter four, information is imperative for developing successful outcomes to a problem. It is also unrealistic to believe that an exchange between cultures would succeed without a major infusion of economic support by the haves to the have-nots.

Collaboration between the peoples of the Islamic and Western worlds is necessary to avert potential tragedy.

Despite the catastrophic consequences of simplistic solutions to complex problems, we continue to behave in a myopic fashion. World history is littered with these instances. A few recent examples include the inadequate development of levees in New Orleans, Louisiana, before Hurricane Katrina; the preemptive strike on Iraq, which the Bush administration claimed would result in world safety; and the fencing-in of Gaza, which Israel believed would make their country safer.

Many of these ideas have failed before. For example, building a wall around Berlin didn't prevent ideas from infiltrating Germany or suppress the will of the East Germans to unite with their brethren in West Germany. Neither did placing Japanese Americans in internment camps make the rest of the US safe. It is perplexing that humankind does not appear to pay attention to its own history. The Maginot Line was a particularly poor strategy by France to defend themselves from attack by Germany. The French believed that by building a well-fortified static line on their northeastern border, they could prevent German forces from entering their country. They never considered that Germany would violate Belgium's neutrality and outflank them through the Ardennes Forest.

Similarly, during the Gulf War, Saddam Hussein's army developed a Maginot-style defense against American forces who were stationed in Kuwait and Saudi Arabia. Even though the US forces had the most highly mechanized and mobilized armada in the history of military operations, the Iraqis dug themselves into fortified bunkers with extensive mine fields to deter the American invasion. The German blitzkrieg of France, though highly mobilized, primarily used tanks. The American blitz, however, was enhanced by technical and scientific breakthroughs led by helicopters that could invade above and around fortifications and were assisted by satellites that could pinpoint enemy positions. Thus, the Iraqi forces were doomed. Furthermore, the immense weaponry of American forces and their allies could turn the Iraq desert into glass, pulverizing the fortifications and the tens of thousands of men within them. Had no one in Iraqi leadership read recent military history? Were they unaware of the US's military might? For that matter, had the US forces not read the history of military failures in Afghanistan, including the Russian catastrophe that led to the collapse of the Soviet Union?

Isn't mental illness doing a single thing that does not work over and over again, believing it will lead to success the next time? Without regard to the stores of information on how to confront the problems attacking society, we are behaving like the Iraqis in the Gulf War, developing static, bunker-like responses to threats.

Since World War II, thanks to research from Weiner, Von Bertanfly, and Bateson, we have understood the complexity and interdependence of systems. Yet despite the proliferation of information and the study of cybernetics, we continue to behave as though social problems are discernible, reducible, and independent of systemic approaches. Most of the thinking in the last quarter century—and possibly throughout the history of the US government—has used one-way causal analysis. The development of education budgets is done independently of strategizing in the Department of Mental Health. The Department of Corrections is asked to work with prisoners and reintegrate them into society without the assistance of corporate America. Likewise, Americans don't understand that cutting taxes results in the loss of social programs and the resulting increase in their insurance bills due to crime and vandalism. There is a basic disregard for ecological philosophy.

Our clinical response to problems is similar to society's responses to threats. Despite the overwhelming data that reveals how the idea of "individual psychopathology" obscures the nature and development of the origins of such problems, we refuse to develop new models for understanding and evaluating these situations. As an aside, it is illusory that individuals exist independent of the systems that support their survival. Certainly, at the family level—if not at the community or society level—individual behavior is in relation to the organization and patterns of significant others. An individual's behavior can't be fully understood without evaluating the interdependence of the family system. Furthermore, the behavior of an individual is not simply a causal response to the behavior of significant others; it is a communication to others as well.

An example of the simplistic ways in which contemporary psychology deals with complex clinical issues is how the educational and mental health communities dealt with this rather usual situation. About an hour after the school day ended, a nine-year-old boy returned to his school and broke all of the windows on the first floor with a baseball bat. The following day, he was excluded from school until he was evaluated for his level of "anger and dangerousness." His mother called the family pediatrician, who in turn referred the family to my practice. The boy's mother told me that her son needed to be evaluated quickly because he couldn't return to school until he was seen by a psychologist.

Much like other clinical examples—possibly due to expediency or theoretical belief—the child was identified as the patient. It would be unusual for an elementary school principal or guidance counselor to tell a mother, "We're concerned about your child *and* your family. We would like you all to be assisted in dealing with this problem." For most clinical situations of this type, the child is brought to a clinic or practice and evaluated on his capability to manage his anger and his feeling states in general. However, in my practice, I invite the family in to begin the evaluation. In this case, I told the mother that I understood her urgency and would make room in my schedule to see her son with the entire nuclear family the next afternoon.

"I guess you didn't hear me," she responded. "I said that my son needed to be evaluated, not me or my family."

"It is our practice to begin the assessment of a child with a family meeting," I replied. "We want to know all of you in the family and understand the family process."

"I'm not coming to any therapy session because my son's a problem," was her retort.

I told the mother then that I would be pleased to assist her but that this was how our process worked. Though clearly irritated, the mother agreed to come the following day.

The next afternoon, I awaited the boy, his parents, and his twelve-year-old brother. However, the parents and the son arrived at the scheduled appointment time without the older brother. When I asked about the brother, the mother responded, "This son is the family problem, not my other boy. I won't subject a good boy to this. One problem in the family is enough."

After the four of us entered my office, I asked the boy if he would consider sitting next to me and being my assistant during the session. He shrugged but nodded in agreement.

"Excuse me, but what are you doing?" the mother asked.

"I need an assistant to help me understand this situation better," I answered.

"My son is a mental problem. How in the world can he help you?"

"I'm not sure, but it is a good sign that he wants to help me!"

It was already clear that more was involved in this family situation than a child who was struggling to manage his anger. His mother, from the initial phone call, had been angry and defensive. His father, on the other hand, hadn't spoken a word. He sat there passively as the session unfolded. The older son was identified as the "good child," yet he was kept at a distance from the evaluation.

Eventually, I turned to the identified child. "Was something happening the day you broke the windows that made you feel angry?"

His mother jumped up and said she had had enough. "Let's go," she said. "We're leaving."

I thought I had missed the boat then. I had not formed an alliance with the power broker in the family, like I had been taught in my postgraduate training. In fact, I seemed to have alienated the mother from my first interaction with her on the phone.

That was when the father spoke up. "Sit down!" he told his wife. "Sit down! I've had enough of this. We've all been frightened to confront you." He turned to me and said, "My wife is a drunk. My boy came home that day and found her out cold on the floor. Sure, he is angry. We're all upset, and I've been afraid to confront her and make her get help."

The boy jumped up from his chair and hugged his father. A process had begun that would bring change to the family. The outcome of treatment included the mother entering a rehab facility as well as the parents' separation and divorce.

The problem of oversimplifying complex situations in clinical cases often leads to little to no movement in the identified problem and, at worst, blaming innocent individuals. The above example is much like many of the clinical problems brought to a therapist. It is only an illusion that individuals exist without correlating, interdependent functions in extended systems such as families. Clinicians must concern themselves with the possibility of doing harm by oversimplifying their treatment modalities. Is it possible that pathologizing individuals only leads to their self-doubt and shame? Or that traditional psychotherapies often result in passivity and dependence? We, as a society, must be concerned about the possibility that traditional ideas and practices in clinical psychology have unintended outcomes that may be destructive to the people it is intended to help.

Chapter Six: Power Over Behavior

Born the son of Cronus, brother of Hestia, Demeter, Hera, Hades, and Poseidon, Zeus was destined to slay his father and become king of the Greek gods. The Titanomachy—or the war between the first and second generations of gods—is deeply ingrained within the psyche of our culture: Zeus not only disembowels his father, but castrates him as well.

It is clear through the earliest cultural myths that power was acknowledged as well as valued as the source of all rightness. After all, it is our culture's tradition that those in power determine the course of societal events and promulgate their philosophy and beliefs. As the saying goes, "History is written by the victors."

Throughout the evolution of our culture, we have been reminded that the powerful can—and will—do what is necessary to maintain control. Among the Germanic peoples, during a ceremony known as a *blot*, sacrifices were made in the name of the god Odin to bring safety and well-being to the land. Slaves were often killed as offerings to Odin. There are even old Swedish tales of the kings Domalde and Olof Trätälja being sacrificed to relieve famine.

In *Civilization and Its Discontents*, Freud concerned himself with the possibility that, without society imposing certain laws and regulations, young men would eventually rise up and kill their predecessors.[1] Power over the behavior of others is possibly the easiest idea to contemplate—and abuse. Dating back to the Greek and Roman civilizations, there is much evidence of extreme cruelty toward those who are less powerful. Though we often celebrate these cultures for their many contributions toward the development of society, we seem to neglect the depravity of some of their actions. Several examples show how the Romans and Greeks demeaned those less powerful than themselves. The Roman emperor Caligula is probably the most blatant example of a leader's destructiveness. He killed his competition—and, though unclear, he may even have killed his parents and his siblings. "Let them hate us as long as they fear us," he said.[2]

During the height of the Roman Empire, the population of Rome grew to almost one million inhabitants. The Romans realized how important their food supply was, since the citizens of Rome often rioted when the food supply was challenged. So they developed scientific farming practices to maximize the production of crops to feed their society. The rules governing farming practices were strictly enforced throughout the empire. One of the principles that was developed was planting crops in rows.

Especially in Judea, farmers were reluctant to comply with Roman regulations. The Jews, during the age of Jesus, were at odds with a culture that codified rules for them that were not promulgated by God.

Of course, the Jews had hundreds of laws, or mitzvahs, to live by without the Romans further complicating their lives. Thus, their farmers protested against Roman authority by refusing to plant their crops in rows. The Romans considered them to be "de liria," or farming out of the rows. The penalty for being de liria was crucifixion. As a result, over 10,000 Jewish farmers were put to death for exercising free practice of their lives. The powerful authorities crucified them because they wouldn't comply with their rules. As Caligula might have concluded, they were put to death because they could be.

Ironically, as Foucault points out in *Madness and Civilization*, the word *delirium* is derived from the ancient term "de liria."[3] Is it possible that we are still using power to coerce those who are different and less powerful than us to think as we do? How often, without reflection, do we cause others in our trust to abandon their ideas or prerogatives and fit our sensibilities? We would all likely agree that the power over a rapist's behavior with an unarmed or weaker woman is a criminal act—or even an act of evil. But how often do we examine our attitudes as teachers, therapists, or parents as we direct our protégés?

Foucault recognized that knowledge itself is a form of power. In 1980, he wrote, "There is an administration of knowledge, a politics of knowledge, relations of power which pass via knowledge and which if one tries to transcribe them, lead one to consider forms of domination by such notions as field, region and territory."[4] The choice and use of language; the use of metaphor; and the elevation of ideas, themes, and paradigms all are political choices that may lead to the subordination and subjugation of alternative constructs. Either intentionally or unintentionally, our development of a thesis limits the direction of potential alternative theses and possible synthesis. Similarly, the degree to which an idea is closely held and dogmatically believed may reduce the amount of room for new ideas and beliefs. Very few original ideas or paradigms for understanding the nature of our intellectual universe (i.e., our world of thoughts and ideas) exist today. Most of our thinking is constructed out of the evolutionary process of previous thinking. The power of culture is to direct the nature of the intellectual discourse based on previous thinking and tradition.

The story that probably has the most impact on any Western culture is the story of Jesus. The idea of power over behavior is deeply embedded within this 2,000-year-old narrative. The concept of evil within Christian theology is also intertwined with the story of Jesus's consideration of power. As the New Testament reveals, Jesus was at odds with the dominant authority of Judaism. In Mathew 23, Jesus states, "The scholars and Pharisees occupy the chair of Moses." The Chair of Moses, a major symbol of Judaism at the time, represented the power and authority to lead the people of Israel. Those who occupied the chair could determine the practice and interpretation of the laws of Moses. Jesus then goes on to say this:

This means you're supposed to observe and follow everything they tell you, but don't do what they do; after all, they're all talk and no action. They invent heavy burdens and lay them on folks' shoulders, but they themselves won't lift a finger to move them. Everything they do is for show. . . . You scholars and Pharisees, you imposters! Damn you! You slam the door of Heaven's domain in people's faces. You yourselves don't enter and you block the way of those trying to enter.

The Pharisees were one of three major sects vying for control of the practice of Judaism at the time. Jesus apparently felt that the dominant narratives of those leading the culture misinterpreted the religion's underlying messages. Thus, he was calling on the people to resist the leadership's cultural imperative. He was seeking to create new space within language and thinking of new interpretations of old ideas. Interestingly, his thinking represents the hermeneutic ideas of postmodern thinking and practice. Through an evolutionary dialogue, he was creating new practices for his culture.

It is clear when a despot such as Saddam Hussein uses power over behavior to control the lives of those he rules. And when a group such as the Kurds of Iraq are massacred for simply being of Kurdish descent, it is a criminal act. We are appalled when we see tribal genocide in Africa and upset to know that individuals are coerced daily into paying tribute to gangs or mobsters. However, do we even notice when our own culture controls the possibility of new ways of comprehending our world through the control of ideas or language—or, for that matter, public policy?

How ironic is it that, since the fourth century, Christianity has been dominated by the same practices as those to which Jesus reacted? Jesus was engaged in a dialogue that challenged the practice of Judaism. Following the times of the bishop Irenaeus of Lyons, ideas challenging the organization of the Christian faith were banished from the culture. Early Christians, in their effort to develop the dogma of their church, refused to consider the possibility of an alternative understanding of Jesus's philosophy. Now, however, the public has been aware of the Gnostic Gospels since the volumes' discovery in Nag Hammadi in 1947. These writings suggest a Jesus who was more mystical in his thinking than the Christian orthodoxy would have us believe.

Recently, the Gospel of Judas was authenticated and now accompanies the Gospels of Jesus's other contemporaries such as Thomas, Mary Magdalene, and Philip. For centuries, Judas had been vilified as one of the evilest and most hated characters in history, since he was often thought of as having betrayed Jesus and caused his crucifixion. But in this new text, Judas is Jesus's most intimate brother. Despite his love of Jesus, Judas obeys the Romans' command and turns Jesus over to the authorities. It is, according to this account, the only way for Jesus to be released from his body and return to God.

It appears that early Christians lost sight of the dialogic nature of Jesus and his disciples. They seemingly didn't understand that form and practice in religion are meaningless without spirituality. But wasn't Jesus's original complaint that the priests of first-century Judaism had lost the essence of their religious practices? Unfortunately, the structure of the emerging Christian culture took on the form and practice of the Pharisees. Wouldn't it be ironic if Jesus were to return today and announce that the priests of contemporary Christianity had gotten it wrong? The emphases of his beliefs were more in line with the Gnostics; even the text of the New Testament was inaccurate.

When studying the Gospels, much of the text has been authenticated through comparison with an ancient Greek text known as *Q*. The following is a statement of Jesus that existed from this ancient manuscript: "Privileged Eyes . . . Turning to the disciples he said privately, 'How privileged are the eyes that see what you see! I tell you many prophets and kings wanted to see what you see; and to hear what you hear, and didn't hear it.'"

Currently, society is witnessing the use of words and language to control the flow of ideas and policy. Within the current worldview, truth holds minimal value. In the contemporary world of politics, the new conservative philosophy of Leo Strauss has taken hold. Strauss believed that any attempt in the modern world to separate facts from values was wrong. He saw himself as a modern-day Socrates. However, one can't study nature without studying human nature as well.

Strauss's view of human nature was at best jaundiced. As he wrote in *The City and Man*, "No bloody change of society can eradicate the evil man; as long as there will be men, there will be malice, envy, and hatred, and hence there cannot be a Society which does not have to employ coercive restraint."[5] His disciples have since had a major influence over George W. Bush and other Republicans. Paul Wolfowitz, former Deputy Secretary of Defense under Donald Rumsfeld, was his student. Other notable followers of Strauss include Richard Perle and Irving Kristol.

Essentially, Strauss was a cross between Plato and Machiavelli. He believed in the idea of philosopher kings but didn't have the patience for the public to learn of the philosopher's correctness. More to the point, he didn't have faith in the nature of the public. They were not to be trusted, in his opinion. He understood that there was conflict that was extant between "the City and the Philosopher." Essentially, the City (or populace) is the Cave in Plato's *Republic*. Strauss believed it was a philosopher's responsibility to say whatever is necessary to achieve the ends that are necessary for the public's interest.[6]

As with ancient Christianity, our modern-day leaders seem to have lost sight of the meaning of their practices. George W. Bush told us that he wanted to spread our democracy to lands such as Iraq. Regardless of this, at least 100,000 civilians died in the process of instituting these "democratic practices." Bush and his administration had not comprehended the magnitude of their destructive decisions. Probably as important is the realization that Bush had adopted Leo Strauss's neoconservative philosophy: to tell the people whatever is necessary to achieve the goals you aspire toward. Giving Bush the benefit of the doubt, let's assume that his actions had the country's well-being at heart. Ideas that might have driven his policies included the need for controlling oil reserves or the belief that protecting multinational corporate interests are the summum bonum of the US government. However, what he told us was often far afield from his underlying concerns.

Would Congress and the American people have supported Bush in going to war in Iraq if he had told them ExxonMobil was concerned about oil prices? How would we have reacted if he had announced that what is good for Halliburton or the Carlyle Group—companies that Bush and his vice president, Dick Cheney, had interests in—was good for the US? In other words, both men used their power to present distorted information and misdirect public attention.

Bush has often been accused of being stupid. However, nothing could be further from the truth. Under the guidance of Karl Rove, his deputy chief of staff, Bush became a master of the use of language. Whenever he was caught in lies, he told the public that either he had misspoken or we didn't understand what he really meant. Time and time again, he ducked under the responsibility for misleading or misdirecting the public. We called him stupid or spoke of him as a "good ol' boy"; in the meantime, he waged war on all who challenged his beliefs. In this way, Bush seems to share in Strauss's perverse notions. To both men, it was important to engage the people in ways that would gain their support. Strauss and Bush believed that evil was a natural aspect of the community. If they didn't control the masses, others who were far more dangerous eventually would. Thus, Bush had become the dangerous, destructive evil he was apparently protecting us from. He and his advisers portrayed themselves as kindly protectors of democracy while they engaged in power over behavior throughout the world.

It is easy to recognize the use of power over behavior. However, it is much more difficult to see how language used by those in control of a culture's institutions often controls the community. Power over behavior instituted in this manner is far more insidious and difficult

80

to contend with than the more blatant examples of a stronger culture enslaving a weaker culture. The world was enraged when Germany invaded the Sudetenland (a region in what is now known as the Czech Republic) or Poland. However, in situations like when the United States declared the Chávez government of Venezuela to be a potential threat to society like Fidel Castro in Cuba, we are placed in a position where defending a government that is concerned with exploiting its people to help multinational corporations is problematic. In this case, coming to Chávez's aid was portrayed as anti-American.

The government's avowed policy is different from its ultimate actions—or even its original intentions. Myriad examples of the duplicitous nature of American policy exist. Whenever the public becomes aware of the government's actual intent, we seem to be inured to the destructive quality of this subversive behavior. Our reaction is often to note that this is how governments do business. In other words, we respond to being bombarded by a culture of language that often obscures reality by closing down and avoiding seeking the truth.

I attended a lecture on the events that had taken place in the northern province of La Guajira, Colombia. Through this lecture, I learned that Colombia was one of the largest coal-producing countries in the world. In fact, coal was the country's leading export. On a related note, here in the US, we have been regularly told that multinationalism is Colombia's appropriate policy. We have been led to believe that the peoples of the world, including Latin America, are the beneficiaries of policies such as the North American Free Trade Agreement, or NAFTA. The US, of course, benefits from low-cost fuel, while the people of Colombia receive needed employment and the benefits of large companies moving to their lands.

However, the actual implementation of policy often goes unnoticed and unexplored. In this instance, the residents of Tabaco, Colombia, were standing in the way of progress. The people of this tiny farm community had lived in peace and relative prosperity for 200 years. They were not interested in moving out of the way of ExxonMobil; and despite years of fighting the claims of powerful companies, Colombia's Supreme Court of Justice ruled that the people of Tabaco were to be relocated.

Unfortunately, the new owners of the Cerrejón open-pit coal mine—Anglo American, BHP, and Glencore—were inpatient with the continued legal haggling by the residents of Tabaco. As a result, paramilitary forces entered the community and bulldozed homes, schools, and a church. The exercising of power over behavior of such incidents is easy to recognize and vilify. However, the lack of discussion of this behavior and the lack of investigation by the power sources exhibiting such behavior go unnoticed. We typically refer to events like those at Tabaco as "collateral damage." And because we have learned the term, we seem to think it protects us from facing responsibility for complicity in policies developed in our name.

Though most people might not suspect that Donald Trump had ever heard of Leo Strauss—or, for that matter, ever read his writings—Trump took the Bush administration's neoconservative style and made it an art form. Before his presidency, he lied about and distorted his wealth to his advantage. Despite being given over $400,000 by his father, he once claimed, "I built what I built myself."[7] And from the beginnings of his public life, Trump had been dishonest about his sexual predilections and business prowess.

Trump's success in both winning the US presidency and conducting himself in office has made it clear that he has moved society into a post-truth era. In November 2018, Glenn Kessler wrote this for *The Washington Post*: "Trump has amassed such a collection of four-Pinocchio ratings . . . as many in his campaign as all other Republican and/or Democrats combined in the past."]p H'isconstituency was fully aware that he wasn't telling truths. They supported (and still support) him, however, because he tapped into their anger. Corey Lewandowski, one of Trump's former aides, once stated, "This is the problem with the media. You guys took everything that Donald Trump said so literally. The American people [don't]."[9] It seems that a large portion of white America is struggling to maintain their power of the quickly growing multicultural plurality.

83

The language of corporate America is similar to that of the government. The intentions of corporate executives often seem to be as much in line with their own wallets as they are with developing directions to benefit their corporations. We are all too familiar with the terrible scenarios at Enron or Tyco. However, what we don't realize is how similar those developments are to the daily practices of executive committees in all of our large companies.

On April 10, 2006, Gretchen Morgenson of *The New York Times* brought an example of such a situation to light. In her article, Morgenson pointed out that while communications giant Verizon had lost 5.5 percent in earnings the previous year, the company's CEO, Ivan Seidenberg, was making $19.4 million in salary and bonuses. This did not include an additional $37 million in stock options. According to Morgenson, Hewitt Associates of Lincolnshire, Illinois had arrived at this executive compensation plan. This company was supposedly an independent consultant to develop "reasonable employee compensation programs." However, Hewitt received $2.8 billion in revenue the year of their consultation with Verizon.[10] Thus, they are neither reasonable nor impartial in developing these compensation programs.

Morgenson's article went on to explain how Hewitt provided actuarial administrative and investment services as well as advice for many Fortune 500 companies, along with providing "independent executive compensation consultation." According to filings with the Labor Department, Hewitt had worked in this fashion for Boeing, Maytag, Procter & Gamble, Nortel, Morgan Stanley, and others. "At Verizon," Morgenson wrote, "Hewitt is ubiquitous. The company operates Verizon's employee benefits web sites where workers get information about their pay, health and retirement benefits, college savings plans and the like"[11] It is clear that the language used by Hewitt—an "objective" consultant—misrepresented the actual relationships between Hewitt and the corporations they consult for. Hewitt depends on executives to hire them to perform the same tasks for their companies that they provide to the executives themselves.

The problem, however, is much more insidious than a CEO receiving too much compensation. Besides stockholders losing money on their corporate shares, about 50,000 middle managers watched as their pensions froze. Additionally, Verizon outsourced the jobs of many operators to India, where their compensation is considerably reduced. And then an internal memo dated April 11, 2006—one day after Morgenson's article was published in *The New York Times*—was sent to Verizon's corporate employees. Their use of language, as usual, was meant to obscure the reality of corporate decision-making. Thus, language was used to maintain the power of corporate leaders over their employees and stockholders.

What follows is an excerpt from the Verizon memo:

Here are our thoughts on [the *New York Times*] article. You may find these points helpful if you supervise employees, and they have questions about the subject:

Verizon has a strong reputation for our exemplary standards for corporate governance, and we emphasize transparency in the executive compensation process. . . .

The article primarily focuses on issues of whether the board of directors of a company should disclose the identity of outside advisers who provide information to a board's executive compensation committee. Verizon does not disclose this information, nor are we required to under SEC guidelines. In fact, the majority of companies in America do not disclose this information.

The reporter made several misleading representations relating to Ivan Seidenberg's 2005 compensation:

For her opening paragraph, the reporter wrote that Ivan Seidenberg's 2005 compensation was 48 [percent] more than in 2004. The actual increase was 12.5 percent.

It was asserted that Seidenberg received $75 million in compensation over the past five years. The actual amount received was substantially less the half of the total cited. . . .[12]

The Verizon memo concluded by saying that Seidenberg actually ranked thirty-seventh among the top 100 CEOs. His compensation package was risk-based and was tied to the company's performance in the future.[13] Thus, the memo wanted Verizon employees to think that the *New York Times* article was exaggerated. It also implied that Seidenberg was expected to achieve his wealth in much the same way those less powerful than him must.

Unfortunately, the Verizon memo didn't address the central concerns of the *New York Times* article. It avoided addressing the huge disparity in power between corporate executives from the working class. It also refused to look at how some people—like the consultants at Hewitt—make astronomical income while the average person loses wages and benefits. Those who are responsible for the welfare of others use language to obscure their intentions and attempt to distract us from the real issues.

The use of language often has unintended implications even in psychotherapy. Clearly, therapists don't intend to dominate their patients. However, as noted in chapter three, even the term *patient* brings with it the implications of being sick or broken. Terms such as *resistant* are regularly used in the taxonomy of therapy. Unfortunately, therapists are often using the power of

their status to double bind the "patient." The individual either agrees with the therapist's assessment or concern or resists it. In either case, the individual is deemed to be the problem.

The situation at Verizon was more than just an abstract concern. The behavior of the executives there came to my attention through the presentation of one of my client's symptoms. This client had been in therapy with me off and on for several years. Originally, she had been seeing me for her experience with anxiety and phobia. During those initial sessions, she sought relief from severe bouts of anxiety around travel. It was particularly difficult for her to fly to regional meetings for her employer, which, of course, was Verizon. She would also experience anxiety from time to time in situations such as the employee cafeteria.

During the first two years of treatment, my client made vast progress. Our discussions during our sessions largely centered on her taking control of her life. She had much difficulty in expressing her anger at superiors, whom she often perceived as lacking creativity and imagination. Over time, she began to assert herself more. She began to trust that her employer—more specifically, her immediate superiors—valued her insight and contribution to the team. As she became more confident in her perceptions and opinions, her anxiety diminished, and my client was promoted to a higher level. But approximately a year and a half later, her symptoms returned.

As I sat with my client and revisited her previous issues and concerns, I wondered what was going on in her life that was once again making her feel powerless and marginalized. The first question

I asked her was rooted in my curiosity regarding the events that had led to her returning to my office. She told me that after eighteen months of anxiety-free travel, she was heading to a meeting in Virginia when she began exhibiting the symptoms of an anxiety attack. "I became short of breath," she explained. "I felt my heart racing, and I was sweating profusely." She couldn't, however, articulate a particular reason for the anxiety attack at this point in her life.

I asked my client if I could question her further on other experiences that were making her feel powerless. At first glance, she seemed bewildered and couldn't connect her feelings during this trip with any events at work or home. Then I asked her if there were any situations or contexts that made her feel victimized or marginalized. She told me that Verizon had just cut back her pension plan. Her expression of anger toward a company that had reduced her future well-being was quite animated. Up to this point, though, she hadn't connected her frustration with Verizon's position on her pension with her latest experiences with anxiety.

Over the next several weeks, I asked my client to research the basis for Verizon's development of this policy on management pensions. The more she discovered, the angrier she became. At one session, she brought her copy of the company-wide memo in response to Morgenson's *New York Times* article. Initially, my client had rationalized that Verizon's pensions might have been hurting the company's capability to compete effectively in "the marketplace." However, she became furious when she realized that her company's CEO was making millions of dollars while her future was in jeopardy. "There seemed to be no sense of fairness or equity in Verizon's position," she said. "Why are we expected to give up so much of our well-being when the company CEO is making excessive profits?" The more my client mused on this, the better she felt. She decided that she needed to start searching for a new job elsewhere while protecting herself at Verizon. Her symptoms quickly evaporated. This made me wonder to what extent other employees at this company were suffering from similar symptoms without recognizing their origins.

The language of therapy is steeped in hierarchy as well as power over behavior. The notion of giving individuals a diagnosis suggests that we are privy to some special body of knowledge that the patient does not possess. We presume that by making the appropriate diagnosis or assessment, we can begin a process of cure and rehabilitation.

The medical model presumes the patient is ill or the problem. This thinking often diminishes the patient's essential worth and value. Of course, therapists want to see themselves as kind and compassionate "healers." But what if people were not considered to be the problem? What if *the problem* was the problem? As Anderson and Goolishian pointed out in *Human Systems as Linguistic Systems*, "[R]eality is a multi-verse of meanings created in dynamic social exchange and conversation."[14] The problems that a patient brings to their therapist then exist in the patient's meaning-making processes and can dissolve through collaborative dialogue. In this case, the therapist can empower the patient to use their meaning-making skills to find new solutions to the problems they are facing. In this way, the therapist does not create through language or practice a situation where the patient is viewed as pathological.

Talking about a patient in therapy not only objectifies that individual but also distances the therapist from a meaningful relationship with the patient. Through dialogue and conversation, the patient may struggle to be understood by their therapist while simultaneously making meaning of them. The clinical language of traditional therapy makes it more difficult for this process of meaning-making to occur. When we talk about patients in terms defined by diagnostic and statistics manuals, we move one step further away from the possibility of true understanding of each other. The emphasis of therapy must be on the development of a collaborative, nonhierarchical relationship. The expert position creates a power-over situation that reduces the likelihood of a safe context for successful meaning-making to occur.

Not long ago, I attended a program developed by the Massachusetts School of Professional Psychology in conjunction with the Boston Psychoanalytic Society & Institute and the Massachusetts Mental Health Center. The program was called the Therapeutic Action of Psychodynamic Psychotherapy: Current Concepts of Cure. The presenters celebrated the fact that they had discovered that the patient-therapist relationship superseded therapeutic interpretation. It was pleasing to see that even psychoanalysts were beginning to understand the power of the real relationship between them and their clients. However, despite this "new and interesting" discovery, they were still talking in ways that diminished the function and participation of their patients. It hadn't occurred to them that using language such as "sadomasochistic style" might damage the well-being of their relationship with a patient. Of course, it was also assumed that doctors can and must discuss their patients in such dismissive terms. Unfortunately, it is also assumed that such terminology is significant to an individual's healing.

In addition, one of the presenters at this program, a well-known psychiatrist from Boston, revealed for the first time publicly that a patient had made her cry. She went on to say that her crying was not out of empathy but out of frustration, and that she had told the patient she was upset she was being treated poorly by her (the patient) and didn't think she deserved this abuse. She had also confronted the patient with the interpretation that the patient was enacting her sadomasochistic relationship with her mother upon the psychiatrist. The psychiatrist then realized that her being so affected by her patient was healing to the patient. She even discovered that more movement in the patient's treatment was coming from the patient's effect on her than perhaps from the interpretation she had given to her patient. Perhaps there would have been an even greater effect had the psychiatrist simply been curious. What if she had asked her patient, "Do you understand why you're choosing to hurt me?" What if she had facilitated the patient coming to her own understanding of her behavior's origins?

In actuality, the term "sadomasochistic enactment" has more to do with maintaining power in the mental health field than it does with the outcome of psychotherapy. In the incident discussed above, the healing came from the patient's awareness of the results of her previously poor behavior. She seemed to notice that her behavior was hurtful and destructive to another individual she cared for. She may even have identified a long-standing narrative dating back to her relationship with her mother that wasn't useful or beneficial to her any longer. What, then, is the purpose of labeling this behavior as "sadomasochistic reenactment"?

My suspicion is that language of this sort not only continues the power differential between psychiatrist and patient but also intimidates other mental health professionals. For decades, the practice of psychoanalysis was only open to physicians. When other professionals were accepted into the analytic societies in the 1970s, those individuals had to sign agreements stating that they wouldn't practice analysis clinically. Today, psychoanalysis is quickly fading from the marketplace of ideas. To give up this language would be tantamount to recognizing that psychotherapy is not a medical profession. Giving up the language of power over behavior would therefore cause a huge shift in the hierarchy of mental health practice.

Chapter Seven: The Convergence

Today, at both the macrolevel of society and the microlevel of community, the world is witnessing problems that are ripe for the development of evil. All around us, situations are unfolding that demonstrate both mischievous behavior and the lack of powerful voices willing to confront this poor behavior. As mentioned throughout this book, the events in the US political sphere are the most blatant and disturbing indicators of the rise of evil. Donald Trump's continuing efforts to manipulate the truth in pursuit of his maniacal aims are the clearest convergence of the four factors that lead to the blooming of evil.

However, many Americans seem not to notice their government's poor behavior in various contexts. Furthermore, the general public appears to be lethargic or complacent in dealing with the convergence of factors that breed evil. From time to time, strong individuals have risen up, willing to confront such construction. Yet today we seem to lack a strong voice or leader who is willing to confront this. The time for such a leader to come forward and prevent a world crisis is quickly emerging.

On February 11, 1898, writer Émile Zola wrote an impassioned defense of Captain Alfred Dreyfus, the highest-ranking Jewish military officer in the French army. The defense, entitled **J'Accuse!,** was written as an open letter to the president of France. Zola was disturbed by the convergence of attitudes that were at the heart of convicting an innocent person. Essentially, Dreyfus was convicted of treason and sent to prison on Devils' Island. His conviction was based on flimsy or nonexistent evidence. Zola recognized that Dreyfus wasn't receiving fair treatment in the French courts because he was Jewish. At the turn of the century, anti-Semitism was prevalent in France. Even the French press had an anti-Semitic bias; and in the case of the Dreyfus affair, the military most likely feared presenting a full airing of evidence that would prove a Jewish man was innocent.

Here, we witness the ingredients for evil once again. Émile Zola confronted all four factors in their convergence:

1. The binary thinking displayed through anti-Semitism

The control of information used by both the military and the press

Simple solutions to complex problems, as seen in a society looking for scapegoats to blame for international espionage

Power over behavior, evidenced in the court's railroading of an innocent man to prison

As Zola wrote to his president in *J'Accuse!*:

And now the image of France is sullied by this filth, and history shall record that it was under your presidency that this crime against society was committed. . . . As they have dared, so shall I dare. Dare to tell the truth, as I have pledged to tell it in full, since normal channels of justice have failed to do so. My duty is to speak out; I do not wish to be an accomplice to this travesty.

Confronting the construction of evil always requires the power and force of truth—at least as best as we can know it to be. In this instance, Zola was referring to hermeneutic truth, or dialogic truth. This concept of truth is evolutionary, never static. It never exists as a set of concrete propositions. Rather, it is contextual and open to new ideas and possibilities. Unlike the concrete propositions of modernistic thinking, where truth is immutable and greater than any location or context, dialogic truth is always open to new understandings and possibilities and can at times appear irrational or contradictory. As is implied in this book's definition in the Introduction to the book truth is often illusive and transitory. However, it is still an admirable objective.

Truth is always one of the first casualties in the war on good and decent behavior. Though truth is always difficult to know, deceit is clear and palpable. Oftentimes those who are seeking personal gain or ways of maintaining their power avoid open and honest dialogue. Instead, they speak in hyperbole and hold disdain for anyone who holds different views or values. Unfortunately, those who sought to have their anti-Semitic views prevail probably murdered Zola. As in other examples of people who confronted the social construction of evil, the forces of the "dark side" always attempt to destroy or discredit those who call for openness and collaboration.

Sir Thomas More illuminated the problem of those who choose to battle evil. To paraphrase him, he once said, "Those who fight the devil, using the tools of the devil become the devil."[1] Thus, the problem for those who seek to create communities of openness and caring is that they fight on an uneven playing field. Good and decent men are often fearful of speaking up and challenging the forces of power and oppression. Even in as blatant an example as the Nazi movement in Germany, most of the culture shrank away from opposing the developing evil. What would the outcome have been different if Hitler had been confronted much earlier in his campaign? As early as 1922, he was making statements that demonstrated all of the ingredients necessary for evil:

If ever I am really in power, the destruction of the Jews will be my first and most important job. As soon as I have power, I shall have gallows after gallows erected, for example, in Munich on the Marienplatz—as many as traffic allows. The Jews will be hanged, one after another, and they will be hanging until they stink. Exactly the same procedure will be followed in other cities until Germany is cleansed of the last Jew![4]

The formation of such repulsive ideas requires the convergence of the four principles of evil we have discussed in this book. It requires the marginalizing and demeaning of those who are unclean or different from us (e.g., creating the inaccurate impression that Jews sacrifice Christians during Passover). It also requires misinformation or the distortion of information regarding the other's position (e.g., the Jews of Germany were rich and powerful and attempting to control the world's wealth). This inevitably requires a simplistic solution to the problem, which Hitler proposed by saying that the Jews would be hanged "until they stink." Even Hitler's statement of the problem ("a world that includes Jews") reeks of evil. Finally, the use of power over behavior by the Nazis to try to exterminate and rid the world of Jewish people was the final ingredient in this convergence of factors that created evil.

Where were the voices of reason as this unfolded? How could such a vile notion be accepted in a culture as sophisticated as Germany? How do we justify our reluctance to intervene in areas where evil is blooming? We seem to prefer blaming outside forces such as Satan or the "axis of evil" instead of confronting our fear or limited behavior. It also must be noted that those in power in society seem to easily consider the use of sophistry (or subtle deception through reasoning) in manipulating others to support their ends. How often did George W. Bush allude to the idea that the people he opposed were similar to the Nazis? Ironically, he set the stage for the likes of Donald Trump, who in turn (and with the assistance of Fox News) turned much of US society into haters who are much like the followers of Nazi Germany.

The character Randle McMurphy, from Ken Kesey's 1962 novel *One Flew Over the Cuckoo's Nest*, was a hero of epic proportions. He stood up to the oppressive power of the mental hospital establishment. In particular, he refused to succumb to Nurse Ratched's domination and sadistic behavior. Here, we once again see a convergence of the factors that foster evil. Though McMurphy is a fictional character, *One Flew Over the Cuckoo's Nest* is based on Kesey's real-life experiences at the Menlo Park VA Medical Center. McMurphy became a celebrated character because he refused to live by the definitions of those who controlled his destiny. He stood up to the professionals who were using—and abusing—their power without caring about how it affected other people.

Let's look at this example from the film adaptation of *One Flew Over the Cuckoo's Nest* where McMurphy stands up to professionals who are objectifying those in their care:

McMurphy: What do you think you are, for Christ's sake? Crazy or something? Well, you're not! You're no crazier than the average asshole out walking around on the streets, and that's it!

Nurse Ratched: Those are very challenging observations you made, Randle.[3]

Here, McMurphy resents the idea that he and other patients are not valued beyond their patient status. The powerful mental health establishment is largely voiced through Nurse Ratched's character. She personifies an approach to treatment that clearly views patients as "less than" those who treat them. She and Dr. Spivey, through their lived experiences, separate themselves by class and qualifications from their "sick patients." Similarly, during a meeting, the institution's doctors recognize that McMurphy is a danger to society but is probably not insane. Nurse Ratched, on the other hand, wants to keep McMurphy in the hospital in the hope of breaking his defiant nature.

Ironically, Dr. Spivey notes the similarities between Nurse Ratched and McMurphy during this meeting:

Dr. Spivey: The funny thing is that person that he's the closest to is the one he dislikes the most. . . . That's you, Mildred.

Nurse Ratched: Well, gentlemen, in my opinion, if we send him back to Pendleton or we send him up to Disturbed, it's just one more way of passing on our problem to somebody else. You know we don't like to do that. So I'd like to keep him on the ward. I think we can help him.[4]

Rather than Nurse Ratched noticing the similarity between herself and her patients, she cruelly distances herself from any meaningful connection to them. As portrayed in Kesey's novel, the language, customs, and hierarchy of the institution's staff allow for the objectification and compassionless treatment of the "mental patients." McMurphy and other patients cease to be understood as humans by the treatment team. The language used by the mental health professionals separates them from those they are treating. Whether through shock treatments, lobotomies, or group therapy, the doctor-patient model requires an "us versus them" stance. Once a doctor views their patient as not being as human as them, their capability to use overly simplistic solutions and the power-over-behavior method becomes easy.

Ironically, it is the dangerous McMurphy who treats his "insane comrades" with kindness and friendship. He beseeches Billy, a timid young man, to get out of the hospital and live his life. "You're just a young kid," McMurphy tells Billy at one point. "What are you doin' here? You oughta be out in a convertible, why, bird-doggin' chicks and bangin' beaver. What are you doin' here, for Christ's sake?"[5]

Ultimately, McMurphy helps Billy take risks and liberate himself from those who are controlling him, including Nurse Ratched and his mother. McMurphy does this by inviting his female friends to the hospital unit and arranging for Billy to make love to one of them. The film then shows Billy's issues dissolving right in front of viewers. We witness as Billy, even momentarily, stops his stuttering. Unfortunately, Nurse Ratched does not seem to notice or care about

Billy's success. She immediately uses threatening and humiliating language to return Billy to his former condition. Billy is so defeated by Nurse Ratched that he eventually takes his own life. Of course, evil is now in full bloom, and McMurphy is the one who is blamed for the tragedy.

Real life often closely resembles what we witness in art. Though labeled fiction, Kesey's novel resonates with readers who have faced out-of-control authority. This situation is often experienced by people who confront large bureaucracies. However, those who seek to do harm or wish for undue power are not the only ones who create problems for other people. Individuals who intend to do the right thing often sow the seeds of evil as well. As seen in *One Flew Over the Cuckoo's Nest*, the daily practices of psychotherapy frequently converge to create destructive consequences for patients. The medical model is clearly intended to result in healing, but the outcome frequently perpetuates self-doubt and concern because the patient often comes to rely on the expert to provide "correct" answers to their questions and concerns.

Unfortunately, all of the factors for creating evil are apparent in this model. The patient role is separated from the doctor role, and the doctor or ancillary medical professional understands themselves to be in a distinctly different class from their patient. Additionally, the language of psychotherapy obscures the meaning of communications between doctor and patient. It is both interesting and peculiar that psychotherapists use inordinately complex language—rather than simple terms—to explain things to patients. Why would one describe a person who sometimes behaves poorly in ways that are uncharacteristic of their usual conduct, or as having superego lacunae?

The therapist has inordinate power in this relationship. Though the therapist is clearly hopeful of doing good and moral deeds, they are rarely open to the patient's challenges of their diagnosis or intervention. So what is the possible outcome of a patient who resists a therapist's interpretations? Might they be described as having a mental illness? A patient who challenges the mental health system is open to similar abuse that McMurphy and his peers received.

Whether it is Zola's challenge to binary thinking or Randle McMurphy's challenge to power over behavior, the forces of power and control can't tolerate those who resist their mandates. They seem to fear a world based on love and caring. It does not matter if the individual confronting them is Salvatore Allende of Chile, who wished to bring prosperity to all in his country; former US president John F. Kennedy, who hoped to bring peace and harmony to the world; Socrates, who challenged the mores of ancient Greece; or Muhammad Anwar el-Sadat, who disputed simplistic answers to difficult political situations. Evil still crops up and attempts to thwart the pursuit of evolutionary change.

Today, we are witnessing a convergence of the conditions for developing evil at all levels of society. In a world of limited resources, we silently watch those in authority accumulate more power and control more of the planet's resources than is fair or reasonable. In 2005, the retiring chair of ExxonMobil, Lee Raymond, received a $400 million retirement package, while most of us paid skyrocketing prices for gasoline. Even now, in the United States, 97 percent of our country's wealth is owned by 3 percent of the population. As during Abraham Lincoln's time, reactionary forces are attempting to maintain an ethos of self-interest and greed. People in power are more interested in economic and material gain than in preserving the environment or caring for others. This included those who conspired to stop Lincoln's attempts to move toward a society based on equality—and their followers are now renewing their efforts to return to a world governed by the privileged aristocracy. Every day, we witness our government obscuring the truth about the motivations for its policies and actions. Fortunately, as a function of the state of communications in society, it has become increasingly difficult for the government to hide its intentions.

How do we make sense of the myriad events taking place around us? Is it not obvious that the conditions necessary to create evil have converged? We are seeing an overabundance of anger and hate as we witness these and other serious challenges to our well-being:

Climate change, the greatest existential crisis of our time, is being downplayed—or, at worse, ignored by much of the population. Ice caps are melting, forests burning, and floodwaters inundating populated areas. Yet our government, as well as major portions of the population, won't react.

Science is being generally rejected by a third of our population. These individuals believe that COVID-19 is a lie, that vaccines can't be trusted, and that biblical narratives are the equivalent of evolutionary theory.

The number of guns now outnumber the US population. It seems like there is a mass shooting almost every day. Children are killed by other children. Militias are threatening to bring order to communities on their terms. People attack other people for alternative beliefs over school board decisions or wearing face masks.

Some individuals believe that there is no truth. From their perspective, the things we are seeing are manipulations by the news agencies. For instance, they believe that we didn't see an insurrection at the US Capitol or the marching of Nazis and white supremacists on the University of Virginia. They also believe that the most successful presidential election in US history was a fraud.

Some also hold the belief that we must stop the "mongrelization" of culture, that only white Christian men should have power. In their opinion, they must do everything they possibly can to suppress women, members of the LGBTQ community, and immigrants.

It is dangerous when community leaders—including politicians and business owners—support untruth and misinformation such as the "Big Lie" of Donald Trump, where he claimed that the 2021 US presidential election was stolen from him. These individuals support their interests over the Constitution of the United States and ethical conduct.

It is my contention that these events meet the definition of evil. And much like the years before Hitler rose to power in Germany, we must act before it is no longer possible for us to change course.

Chapter Eight: The Special Problem of Physiology

Frequently, I'm asked about the idea that certain people are evil as a result of biological impairment. Hasn't modern medicine identified portions of the brain that are associated with anger and violence? For example, aren't certain parts of the limbic system associated with severe aggression? Aren't there individuals who are so evil and heinous that they are clearly physiologically broken? Though the answer is an emphatic yes, the number of people who meet the standard of evil by way of neurological or physiological impairment is negligible.

The reality is that these individuals are not society's major concern. Despite the efforts of modem medicine to proffer solutions to the world's ills, it has mostly offered false hope. The millions of dollars thrown away on research to establish the physiological causes of evil would have been better spent on the education and development of those who are disenfranchised in their communities and who mostly cause violence. Even the hoopla over medicines to reduce psychiatric symptoms is mostly hype—and not even good science.

Over the forty years I have been in practice, I have seen hundreds of families and thousands of individuals. However, less than a handful of these people appeared to have had an "evil disorder." Clearly, no one who appeared in my office with such a condition would ever be considered for local office, let alone head of state. Likewise, we would never have found Saddam Hussein, Adolf Hitler, or Judas Iscariot to have met the standard for diagnosis of this condition. And it is only possible—maybe even probable—that Jeffrey Dahmer or Dennis Rader (aka the BTK Killer) had physiological aberrations that would have met this standard.

Despite the interest of cable news and the Internet, physiological dysfunction makes up a small portion of the world's evil. Furthermore, biological impairment is the source of only a small percentage of poor behavior. The real culprit to poor behavior in society and the evil perpetrated in our communities is the social construction of destructive ideas and stories by the evildoers. It is the confluence of the four conditions discussed earlier in this book— binary thinking, control of information, simplistic solutions to complex problems, and power over behavior—that lead to the construction of narratives vested in evildoing.

When one reviews the history of medical causes of mental illness, especially studies in violence and aggression, one will find a litany of misadventures. The discovery of Thorazine, for instance, was accidental. In 1950, French scientists at Rhône-Poulenc's laboratories who were working on a substance to treat nausea noticed that this substance tranquilized the patients. Thorazine (or, more correctly, chlorpromazine) was the first phenothiazine marketed by GlaxoSmithKline as an antipsychotic. No one at the time would have predicted the long-term damage this chemical would do to the patients who would use it. Today, Thorazine is used only on a limited basis because of its extrapyramidal side effects. The drug causes tardive dyskinesia, which is characterized by rhythmical, involuntary movements of the tongue, face, mouth, or jaw and sometimes by involuntary movements of the extremities and a peculiar gait.

When chronicling medical misadventures in controlling poor behavior, we must review the history of psychosurgery, which is still being researched at universities such as Harvard. Surgeons have been drilling holes into other people's heads for almost 7,000 years. However, the first modern attempt to control aggression through surgery was done at the University of Lisbon in 1935. A procedure known as a prefrontal lobotomy, where the connections between the prefrontal cortex and the rest of the brain were severed, was instituted. In the early days of lobotomies, holes were drilled into a person's head in much the same way our ancestors had. Then a wire would be inserted, severing connections in the brain. The procedure was perfected by Walter J. Freeman by inserting an ice pick into the orbit of the eye, then swinging it back and forth, severing brain connections. No surgical scars were necessary.

Our (fictional) friend Randle McMurphy wasn't the only patient to be lobotomized. Between 40,000 and 50,000 patients received lobotomies in the 1940s and 1950s. It seemed that modern medicine had perfected the cure to one's foolish behavior. But it eventually became clear that medicine's pursuit of cures to evil and out-of-control behavior was barbaric and cruel. The victims of lobotomies were often left listless and without motivation, losing their identities to modernism.

Trying to find evil within a person's physiological makeup is mostly an exercise in futility. Modernism—or at least modern medicine—would have us believe that all of our psychological and spiritual functions can be located within particular synaptic functions of the cerebral cortex. Though I wouldn't disagree about the reality that all human function has biological correlates, how we function is much more complex than mapping specific sites in the brain with specific thoughts and actions. The idea of the existence of particular structures of the body is a useful metaphor, but it is not a truth.

When I was studying neurophysiology in graduate school, my classmates and I had large atlases of the brain that located particular regions of that organ. We would then identify specific functions of the human experience to the site illustrated in the atlas. My peers and

I were wrong in those assumptions. Today, clinicians recognize the cybernetic nature of brain functioning. Through the use of PET scans, we can watch as multiple sites in the brain become involved with an individual's complex functions. Only recently have we begun to believe that a person's brain functions are inextricably interrelated with hormonal functions. In fact, all of the body is interdependent. The heart can't function without the brain and vice versa. We can orchestrate thoughts and feelings by touch, smell, or even memory. The mind, in its complexity, is greater than any other organ system or bodily functioning. Thus, the whole of human experience is greater than its parts. Modernism once again leaves us believing in answers and truths that are too often simplistic.

Continued research on human anatomy and function is undoubtedly important. However, the hope of reducing evil and poor behavior through convenient medical intervention may be senseless. In 1984, *The New England Journal of Medicine* devoted an entire edition to the concept that the use of hypnosis in cancer treatment amounted to quackery. It debunked the idea that tumors could be reduced through hypnotic imagery. They particularly skewered the Symingtons, noted psychologists in Arizona who were treating cancer patients through imagery. The irony was that this edition of the famed medical journal spurred research efforts to understand the interrelationship between mind and body. An entire new field of study known as psychoneuroimmunology emerged.

Researchers at the Massachusetts Institute of Technology and Beth Israel Deaconess Medical Center in Boston demonstrated the complex interactive effect of being in a hypnotic state with the attachment of norepinephrine on receptor sites of killer T cells. It was their understanding that norepinephrine enhanced the ability of T cells to attack cancerous tumors. They discovered that patients who were in a relaxed state had significantly more norepinephrine in their blood. Thus, patients receiving hypnosis were more likely to improve than those in control groups.

Science, and medicine in particular, has contributed to the well-being of our communities. So it is not my intention to dismiss our efforts to better understand the complexity of our lives, nor to say that research is unnecessary or unwanted in the pursuit of a better quality of life. However, the problem is that, as part of their efforts to maintain power and control, various forces in our communities misuse science for their ends. In particular, the use of simplistic ideas to confront society's ills needs to be addressed. This notion is paramount to the idea that we can locate evil in our genetic construction.

Evil is much more readily seen in pharmaceutical companies than in the human body. In this particular industry—a multibillion-dollar business vested in the concept that life's problems of life are fixed through taking pills—one can frequently witness the convergence of factors that lead to evil. This industry is continuously stating that medicine is the best hope for humanity. And today, three times as many children are taking psychotropic drugs as there were ten years ago. To psychiatrists, it is apparent that they are no longer curing mental illness but rather ameliorating unpleasant symptoms. However, they continue to conspire with pharmaceutical companies to maintain the belief that medicine is necessary to cure mental problems. In fact, these companies and the American Psychiatric Association have joined with large advertising firms to maintain economic advantage and ultimate power in the mental health field.

Research study after research study emphasizes just how complex the process of creating significant change in the lives of people who exhibit psychological difficulty can be. Real change comes through a process that often includes individual therapy, family and community change, and medicine. However, thanks to high-powered marketing strategies and advertising campaigns, the general public is often duped into believing that their problems—as well as the problems of those they love, particularly their children—can be fixed by taking medicine. Millions of individuals are now taking prescriptions that are unnecessary or insufficient in bringing them significant relief from their problems.

One issue that has emerged over the past few decades is the use of Prozac and other selective serotonin reuptake inhibitors (SSRIs) in children. Unfortunately, in their zeal to sell medicine to the public, pharmaceutical companies often don't do the appropriate research. The situation is even worse than SSRIs being ineffective or inadequate for relieving anxiety or depression. In his book *Prozac Backlash*, Joseph Glenmullen, MD, notes that the long-term side effects of SSRIs on children can be disfiguring and debilitating. Children can develop symptoms ranging from neurological disorders, whole-body tics, and mild leg tapping to severe panic, muscle spasms, and bizarre posturing.[1]

Similarly, in February 2004, Dr. Jane E. Garland, head of a clinic for mood and anxiety disorders at a children's hospital in British Columbia, Canada, reported that antidepressant medications have minimal to no effectiveness in childhood depression. As Carey Goldberg wrote in 2004 for *The Boston Globe*, "Worse than the fact that the results of Dr. Garland's study challenged the efficacy of the use of these medicines with children is the realization that she was restrained from reporting them by a nondisclosure agreement with the pharmaceutical maker."[2]

In April 2004, the British medical journal *The Lancet* also criticized pharmaceutical companies for not publishing studies that showed a high suicide risk in adolescents who were taking SSRIs. David Healy, MD, is probably one of the leading historians on the use of psychotropic medication. He has been an active researcher and advocate for the use of medicine. However, in an article of his that was published in *Psychotherapy and Psychosomatics* in 2003, Healy reported that he believed the risk of suicide was at least double that reported by the pharmaceutical companies. He also wrote that he didn't believe enough research had been compiled by the US Food and Drug Administration on the safety of this medicine for children and adolescents. As an aside, Healey noted that when Eli Lilly and Company originally developed Prozac for the marketplace, it was designed to be an antianxiety agent. But at the time of its creation, it didn't compete favorably with Valium and was remarketed as an antidepressant. Thus, this class of medicine was never intended to be an antidepressant, let alone be used by children.[3]

Likewise, in June 2004, a group of noted therapists under the auspices of the Alliance for Human Research Protection (AHRP) wrote a letter to Thomas R. Insel, MD, head of the National Institute of Mental Health (NIMH), with a copy sent to Tommy Thompson, then-Secretary of Health and Human Services. The letter was entitled "Published NIMH Prozac Trial Report Concealed Suicide Attempts by Teenagers." This group of therapists included Loren Mosher, MD; Sally Rosgow; and Ed Hassner Sharav. In this letter, David Cohen, PhD, and Vera Sharav, president of the AHRP, were essentially accusing the federal government of colluding with the pharmaceutical industry in fraud. They noted that when *The New York Times*—as well as other news sources—asked questions on whether the negative trials were concealed by Eli Lilly and Company, the lead researcher, Dr. Graham Emslie, refused to comment. The introduction of the AHRP's letter states the problem with medical/pharmaceutical research best:

Recent revelations indicate that pharmaceutical companies selectively reported partial (favorable) clinical trial results from pediatric antidepressant trials and concealed evidence of harm from physicians, other health care professionals and the public. It is universally agreed in the literature that failure to disclose all trial results compromises physicians' ability to provide professional care—thereby increasing the likelihood of causing preventable harm. More generally, failure to disclose trial results in scientific publications taints the scientific literature (by rendering it not credible) and, as New York State attorney Eliot Spitzer charged recently, constitutes plain and simple fraud.[4]

It is alarming to realize that rich and powerful organizations conspire with scientists and the regulating agents who are responsible for protecting us. The situation is ripe for evil-making. These groups have no awareness of the reality of those individuals who need relief from anxiety and depression. Their goal seems to be to create markets for selling their wares. In their opinion, we the public are a class of people who are separate from the corporate entity and its shareholders—yet another example of binary thinking. Furthermore, the pharmaceutical industry conspires to maintain control of information and share only the facts that maximize their economic position. Through clever marketing and advertising, they offer simple solutions to complex human dilemmas. Finally, through the use of economic power, they attempt to control society and its agents, With hundreds of millions of dollars, this is how the pharmaceutical industry indoctrinates the public.

Let me share a story from my past that illustrates the arrogance of modern medicine. About thirty years ago, I met with the chief physician of a small community hospital. At the time, psychologists were being given hospital privileges for the first time. I hoped to demonstrate to this chief physician the services my colleagues and I could perform at his hospital. But during our meeting, he wondered out loud, "What could a psychologist do for his patients that he couldn't do himself? My patients come to me for all sorts of problems. They look to me for my wisdom. By the way, this wisdom was achieved through having gone to medical school and treating many patients. Do you really think you can offer to my patients what I do?"

My response lacked wisdom but underscored my academic training: "There is a great deal of research that demonstrates that patients come to their physician for support and caring. Talcott Parsons, the great sociologist, noted that many people come to the physician's office simply to be touched. These people often don't require the sophisticated medical training of the doctors of the medical staff. They require a warm and comforting response from an empathic listener. It's probably more useful for you and your colleagues to treat their physical illness, and for my cohorts and I to take care of their personal problems."

The chief physician thought for a second before saying, "It probably wouldn't be useful to give you privileges. But if you liked, I would consider hiring you in my office, and you could work for me."

I imagined the economic wheels that were likely spinning in his head. The psychologist down the hall would be a new profit center for him. He could offer his patients a new service and never give up control.

The irony was that, ultimately, the chief physician was correct. He, along with most other compassionate and collaborative listeners, could provide valuable assistance to others. Again, it is not my intention to suggest that training for counselors is not useful. However, that training should be mostly in communication and listening skills. A counselor's expertise is in providing a mechanism for change in the client's problem, not in special knowledge of the client. The chief physician, however, couldn't get past his own pride long enough to care about sharing the responsibility of caring for those in his trust with clinicians in my field.

This book is not intended to be a condemnation of psychology, science, medicine, or psychiatry. One of the prime considerations of this argument, however, is that black-and-white thinking (i.e., binary thinking) is one of the currents that lead to evil. Totalizing thinking is black-and-white in nature. Here in the twenty-first century, it is clear that the advancements of science and medicine have done great good for humanity. The Human Genome Project in particular has made it possible to treat individuals with genetic disorders and make individualized medicine possible.

The vast amount of research that has taken place over the last ten years has made the creation of the COVID-19 vaccine possible. (How ironic it would be for this discussion of the medical community's pitfalls to be ammunition for anti-vaxxers?) Though one could commiserate with those individuals who are also troubled by the pharmaceutical industry's past wrongs, the overwhelming evidence is that hundreds of millions of applications demonstrate that the COVID-19 vaccine works and is safe. And yet, in the midst of a pandemic, an issue of great importance to the world is being politicized by those who are only interested in making mischief—or, worse yet, destroying the well-being of their communities. Unfortunately, once again we are seeing the seeds for evildoing being planted.

Chapter Nine: Fundamentalism, or the Age of Dogma

Ironically, both fundamentalism and postmodernism are reactions to the conditions of the modern world. It seems that the ethos of capitalistic consumption has failed many in Western culture as well as the Islamic community. Individuals all over the globe are becoming increasingly distrustful of the values that so blatantly despoil our Earth and use its resources so unevenly. Postmodernists and religious fundamentalists are also equally concerned with the directions in which our global leadership is taking us.

However, it seems that the two philosophies' modern capitalistic values diverge after their shared concern with narcissistic self-indulgence. Postmodernism honors curiosity, new possibilities, and evolutionary change. It is rooted in a community ethos in which caring for each other and our world is paramount. Fundamentalism, on the other hand, is built on long-standing, unalterable "truths." It discredits ideas that challenge its basic tenets. Any questioning of its rules and mores is seen as apostate—or even evil. Fundamentalists are frequently willing to use any means, including death and destruction, to stop practices they believe to be incorrect. From this perspective, it seems that fundamentalist beliefs are consistent with the convergence of the four factors that lead to evil.

121

The term *fundamentalist* was originally used by the Bible Institute of Los Angeles in 1909. They published four volumes of books known as *The Fundamentals*, which were sent to all of the Protestant ministers throughout the United States. The concern behind these volumes was the developing modern practice of Christianity. The hope was to return Christian doctrine to "fundamental" issues such as the Virgin Birth and the resurrection of Jesus. Essentially, fundamental Christian doctrine views the Bible as being divinely inspired and infallible.

Interestingly, despite the clash between Christianity and Islam that is taking place today, both Islamic and Christian fundamentalism share the belief that Allah (or God) revealed himself through ancient text. Islamic fundamentalists believe that one should understand the Quran and the hadith literally. Much like their Christian counterparts, they advocate a political reality based on theological law. Both Christian and Islamic fundamentalists see their struggle with modernity to be of major importance. In their minds, the world's future well-being depends on their view of community life prevailing.

At first, it may seem that postmodernism accepts the views of fundamentalists. However, fundamentalists refuse to live in a world where others question their views or live their lives with alternative value systems. A postmodernist would probably not choose to live their life on a fundamentalist's terms but rather to coexist with those who practice this way of being. Fundamentalists, on the other hand, assume that those who identify as members of the LGBTQ community, have abortions, or practice birth control are practicing evil. Some fundamentalist groups even believe that it is their responsibility to convert everyone to their belief system.

For instance, Christian fundamentalists of today resent the teaching of Darwinism. They believe that creationism is on equal footing with evolutionary biological theory. Thus, they make every effort to change the nature of teaching science in our schools to include their ideas. School boards in Kansas and Pennsylvania have attempted to enact legislation that only science books including creationism should be used in their schools. Fundamentalists such as Osama bin Laden and George W. Bush have even been willing to go to war to propagate their belief systems.

Obviously, fundamentalist ideals are the major challenge to a world of ever-changing, developing knowledge. How do we have a dialogue with individuals who profess that dinosaur bones were placed here by God to fool us about the true nature and time of creation? How do we face the challenges to society when Tom DeLay, who was the House Majority Leader for part of Bush's presidency, had a sign on his wall that read, "This could be the day"? What does it portend to the world that former US presidents George W. Bush and Donald Trump don't believe in global warming? More recently,

Christian fundamentalists gained control of the Republican Party in the United States. These Republicans, who were in power in all the branches of the federal government, believed they would return to power in the next election. They seemed to be driven at least in part by End Time prophecies from the Bible. They also ignored global warming and fuel resources because they had faith that the Rapture was coming. Isn't it odd that Republican administrations that were once concerned about the development of theocracies in the Middle East now seem to be moving in that direction at home?

From the beginnings of the United States, tension has existed between those who wanted a government rooted in Scripture and those who wanted a government rooted in freedom. Today, we are witnessing Puritans ascend to positions of control in the country. The vision of former Massachusetts governor John Winthrop as shared in his famous speech, "City on a Hill," is finally coming into fruition:

For we must consider that we shall be as a city upon a hill. The eyes of all people are upon us. So that if we shall deal falsely with our God in this work we have undertaken, and so cause him to withdraw His present help from us, we shall be made a story and a by-word through the world.[1]

The problem, of course, is that since the seventeenth century, society has become increasingly pluralistic. The United States no longer has a white Protestant majority. Two hundred years have passed since the arrival of the Puritans, and we now pride ourselves on being a "melting pot" society. We celebrate the values inscribed on the Statue of Liberty:

. . . "Give me your tired, your poor,

Your huddled masses yearning to breathe free,

The wretched refuse of your teeming shore.

Send these, the homeless, tempest-tost to me.

I lift my lamp beside the golden door!"[2]

However, the problem is greater than religious practice. Fundamentalism is at the heart of the struggle between those who are aiming for an inclusive society and those who wish to maintain a white Protestant-dominated culture. The anger demonstrated at the US-Mexico border is a reflection of the deeply held beliefs of the separate forces of pluralism and ethnocentrism. Groups such as the Minuteman Project, who assist Border Patrol in guarding the US-Mexico border, protest that it is their concern to keep our country a land of laws. The anger of this group, and the concomitant rage of Mexican Americans at their presence, suggest a pro-white bias on Minuteman's part.

The discrepancy between the Republican and Democratic parties is another example of the struggle between those who are concerned with sameness and those who believe in diversity. The Republicans emphasize a theory of limited government. They advocate for lowering taxes and limiting the functions of the federal government. Yet today they have become instrumental in developing laws for the government's intrusion into the lives of US residents. Not only do they advocate for moral codes that would limit the freedom of the LGBTQ community as well as women's reproductive rights, but they have also expressed a desire to develop police forces for monitoring people's lives. The Republican Party has become the party of those who fear threats from within and without our borders. These politicians have come a long way from being the party of Abraham Lincoln. They have become the party of "security" rather than one of freedom.

The Democratic Party, on the other hand, has become the party of those who desire to be open and inclusive. It consists of diverse constituencies who have little in common except their tolerance for each other. These include groups of individuals who are often feared or loathed by those in the Republican camp. Groups within the Democratic Party range from those who support the rights of LGBTQ families to those who welcome non-whites into their communities. As with the case of postmodernists, the Democrats are often accused of being valueless.

The tension in US politics has become massive. People often discuss the situation as a struggle between the red states and the blue states. Though we regularly perceive the national dichotomy as between the coastal states and the country's midsection, in actuality the division exists everywhere. Red and blue counties can be found in every state. The urban, more diversified areas of society often struggle with the rural, more insular regions. In Texas, a deep red state (and the home of George W. Bush), the city of Houston is one of the most liberal and diversified cities in the country. Similarly, the Commonwealth of Massachusetts—home to US Senator Elizabeth Warren and frequently considered the most liberal state in the country—has a large population of extremely conservative residents who are enraged at the thought of gay or lesbian marriage. It appears that we are in the midst of a theoretical civil war between those who would prefer to be governed by Christian fundamentalism and those who wish to continue an inclusive democracy. The ideas that separate the right and left wings have brought the population to loggerheads with each other. Not since the American Civil War has there been as large and vociferous a debate between opposing thought systems.

At the microlevels of US society, one can find a reflection of the broader societal struggle. Many of today's psychotherapists are concerned with practices in our profession that don't appreciate or honor polyvocality. Unfortunately, psychotherapy has a long tradition of seeking dogma to guide it. Beginning with Freudian psychology, there has been a cult of sameness and continuity that has often lost sight of meaningful innovation in lieu of reproducible practice. Freud himself was open to ideas and practices that were dissimilar to those his protégés demanded of one another.

In his case studies, Freud didn't necessarily use the proscribed techniques of the cult that followed him. He wasn't bound by the structure of those who later practiced psychoanalysis. His theory of infantile sexuality was based in part on his correspondence with the father of Little Hans, who was also a physician. His musings on paranoia and homosexuality were developed from the case of Daniel Paul Schreber, a German appeals court judge. Freud's ideas were based on Schreber's account of his own illness. These and other similar cases were not stylized or rigidly structured by the forms of Freud's later disciples. Freud himself brought a degree of creativity, thoughtfulness, and curiosity to psychotherapy that was apparently lost on those followers. He listened thoughtfully to the people he assisted. Clearly, the most dogmatic of theories in the field of psychotherapy missed the beauty and wisdom of its founder. Isn't it ironic that Freud's disciples were so determined to make psychoanalysis a science that they instead created a meaningless taxonomy? Because these individuals were physicians, they were determined to create a body of knowledge that was based on verifiable facts.

128

However, it seemed lost on Freud's disciples that there was no such entity as an ego—or, for that matter, any of the other structures outlined in psychoanalytic theory. Ego is a metaphor, a linguistic tool that is often helpful in communicating ideas about the human function. The more determined we are to force an idea on ourselves, the more likely we are to set ourselves on a fool's journey. As Wittgenstein noted in 1931, "Language sets everyone the same traps: it is an immense network of easily accessible wrong turnings. And so, we watch one man after another walking down the same paths and we know in advances where he will branch off, where walk straight on without noticing the side turnings, etc. etc. . . . "[3]

Psychologists spent much of the twentieth century aligning themselves with one theoretical camp or another. Much like the religious struggle in society, these fundamentalist positions may have been interesting but not truthful. Each of these basic traditions of psychology (e.g., ego psychology, behaviorism, cognitive behavioral therapy, existential, and physiological) took an either-or orientation to one another. They struggled to prove themselves to be correct while attempting to disprove the others. The time has come for us to take a both-and orientation to the world of psychology. Furthermore, it is important to understand that psychologists' ideas can exist in offering us useful directions but that there are limits to our understanding. Efforts to codify psychology beyond these limits may actually be destructive to those we intend to help.

In the instance of psychotherapy, the lenses a therapist brings to a therapy session have often precluded them from hearing issues that are important to their clients. As Gergen and Kaye pointed out in *Therapy as Social Construction,* the unintended outcome of misunderstanding a client's concerns is a consequence of attributing theory before listening to those who are seeking our assistance. Depending on their therapeutic posture, therapists may find themselves moving in directions that are predetermined by their theories.[4]

Unfortunately, this can be destructive to the lives of patients. In the instance of society as a whole, Burge noted in *The New York Times* that secular Americans grew from 5 percent in the 1970s to 30 percent during the years of Donald Trump's presidency. However, during the Trump years, there was no decline in evangelicalism. Interestingly, Burge also noted that this wasn't because those self-described fundamentalists had become more involved in the divinity of Christ, but because they highly identified with the gospel of the Republicans. Nonattendance at church services rose from 16 percent in 2008 to 27 percent in 2021.[5] Evangelicals may not have become united in their religious beliefs, but they are united in their support of Republican fundamentalism.

The cure to fundamentalism is dialogue. Whether in politics, religion, or psychotherapy, being open to an inclusive dialogue is the essential ingredient to defeating the forces of static belief. We must promote situations that allow for listening to one another. No single belief system holds all the variables for the constructive development of civilization.

We must continue to develop those mechanisms that promote active listening in society. In psychotherapy, the promulgation of witness and reflection teams has been an innovation that has increased the patient's sense of being heard during their treatment. It has also increased the client's sense of acknowledgment and personal safety.

The basis of this process is that the reflecting team bears witness, then repeats the client's message back to them without judgment. The client listens to the reflecting team and determines whether their point has been heard and understood. For many patients, there is also a secondary effect of feeling as though they are being listened to and moving others. The reflecting team then provides examples from their own lives in which the client's position has validity. From there, patients often develop a sense of agency.

Chapter Ten: Sexual Perversity

When discussing evil, people frequently ask me to explain the "bad behavior" of pedophiles, rapists, and other sexual deviants. The questions they post most often are, "Aren't they truly evil? Aren't they examples of people who are naturally tainted?" It seems that almost every day, we have to talk about sexual behavior gone amuck in our communities. Not long ago, newspapers in the Boston area were full of articles suggesting that the head of Boston's Catholic hospital system has been sexually harassing female employees. At the time, Dr. Robert M. Haddad was about to be terminated from his position as president of Caritas Christi Health Care. Shortly after that, television and print news media began reporting on congressional hearings regarding sexual predators on the Internet.

Similarly, the Clinton presidency was destroyed by years of debate and trial around whether to impeach US President Bill Clinton over poor sexual behavior while in the Oval Office. Most recently, the Pope apologized for the cover-up of tens of thousands of instances of pedophilia by priests in France.

Every day, an estimated sixty-eight million requests are made for pornographic material on the Internet. In 2015, *Psychology Today* reported that there were two billion uses of the Internet for pornographic material. This number represents 25 percent of all daily search engine requests. Additionally, approximately seventy-two million people visited adult pornography sites in 2004, and over $12 billion in revenue was generated from Internet pornography in 2005.[1] This number is greater than the profits generated from all of the major broadcasting companies combined.

Do these facts imply that our community has become possessed by the devil? Do these examples of poor sexual behavior by our leaders and ourselves prove that we are a perverse, evil society? And if wickedness does not reside in these individuals, then what is at the core of this behavior?

As a psychologist, I'm frequently confronted by people who are fearful of pedophiles in our midst. At lectures, in community meetings, and in my office, parents want to know how to protect their children. They are dreadfully concerned about people in their community who might exploit their children sexually. What most people don't realize, though, is that the greatest danger to children comes from their family members or other individuals they are already familiar with—in other words, the very people we expect to guide and protect our children.

In a study conducted by Survivor Connections, a sexual abuse research group based in Cranston, Rhode Island, only 364 out of almost 3,000 children who were victims of sexual molestation had been harmed by unknown perpetrators. Family accounted for 704 of the total incidents, neighbors and family friends for another 199, Roman Catholic priests for 994, and non-Catholic clergy members for an additional 217 cases.[2] Similarly, the Wisconsin Coalition Against Sexual Assault reported that 46 percent of children who are rape victims have been assaulted by a family member.[3]

What are the implications of these statistics? Even though the problem of poor sexual behavior exists mostly within families, Congress, the media, and society in general seem to be scared that our children are in danger from some unknown outside source. Once again, evil is understood as residing in "them" and not in "us." Despite research and literature that proves the contrary, we behave as though we are not aware of the evidence of the real dangers around us. We look for simple solutions, then wish to eradicate the problem. We create watch lists of those who have committed sexual crimes as if to say, "Let's round up the perverts and isolate them from our community."

From the above example and myriad other data, it seems that the sexual mores that were established thousands of years ago are no longer useful or working. An estimated three-fourths of all married men and over a third of all married women have had extramarital relationships. Perhaps the sexual rules of our culture have never worked from our culture's inception. Despite the overwhelming data that society is at best sexually adrift, we continue to preach ideas about sexual fidelity and commitment as though these ideas are functional. Isn't it ironic, then, that fundamentalist preachers such as Jimmy Swaggart and Jim Bakker are among those who have betrayed their professed teachings? In my own practice, I have treated many clergy members who have maintained poor boundaries with their congregants.

As noted in chapter one, in the story of creation, the ancient Hebrews decided to abridge the story of Adam and Eve. Rather than address their awareness of the challenge of creating a society in which male-female relationships were fraught with complexity and difficulty, they ignored the problem. Thus, the most interesting and informative portion of the story—the relationship between Adam and Lilith—was excluded from the Bible.

Interestingly, the ancient biblical text includes the story of David and Bathsheba. David, a king of Israel, was considered to be the greatest of God's children. However, not only did he have a sexual liaison with the beautiful Bathsheba, but he also conspired against her husband, Uriah. In other words, David had an affair with another man's wife, impregnated her, and then had her husband killed. However, David was considered to be such a pious figure that Jesus himself was supposedly descended from the king's house. Though the narrative of David and Bathsheba is included in the Old Testament, the explanations of the story and the couple's behavior are unsatisfying.

Reb Nachman of Breslov, great-grandson of the founder of Hasidism, explained that it was God's will that David behave poorly with Bathsheba: "The truth is that David was such a holy person that by nature, he could not have sinned at all. God forced him, as it were, to sin in order that he would serve as an example for all of humanity."[4] Additionally, there is a dispute in the Talmud as to whether Bathsheba was actually married. The Talmud rules that she wasn't, since law at the time required that soldiers divorce their wives before going to war. The idea was to allow for a woman to be free in the case that her husband died in battle. It seems that religion has great difficulty in dealing with male instincts. Many stories that suggest the difficulty of dealing with sexual tension are either removed or explained through teachings such as Reb Nachman's theory.

Judaism goes to elaborate lengths to explain the behaviors of those who are mostly admired but sometimes function outside the culture's expressed practices. Why is it not enough to note that an individual's behavior and motives are often more complex than we would have them be? Though the tradition of one man and one woman was clearly established within the Old Testament, several biblical figures had more than one wife. Most of these men had wives serially. However, in Genesis 16:2, Sarah gave her husband, Abraham (and the father of

Judaism, Christianity, and Islam), permission to engage in sexual relations with her handmaiden, Hagar. Similarly, King David had multiple wives, and concubines as did King Solomon.

It seems that somewhere in ancient biblical times, the question of sexual relations became intertwined with the problem of material ownership. Throughout the Bible, women are discussed as being the property of men. In fact, injuring a woman required proper compensation to her husband and not directly to her. Additionally, throughout the Book of Exodus, there are examples of men having ownership of their women. Male servants could be given wives by their masters; however, there are no references to the opposite being true. In Exodus 21:25, the text states that if a pregnant woman is injured in a fight, her husband is to be compensated for the hurt inflicted upon her. And in the Book of Deuteronomy, the text suggests that adultery is only between a man and another man's wife. Sex with a concubine or prostitute is acceptable. Though we have constructed a series of moral rules to guide us based on biblical text, we seem to not have paid close attention to the struggles of the individuals within that text. Thus, we have ignored the instinctual proclivity of those who are involved in the super narrative of our time.

It seems that the culture's major concern is maintaining the power structure of the community. The laws of ancient Judaism, as with the myths that have been incorporated into our collective imagery, are dominated by ideas where men have power over women. For instance, a man can have more than one sexual partner, but a woman can't. Until recently, community laws have diminished the power and value of women. (At this point, women have had the right to vote for less than 100 years.) Remember that, as stated earlier in this book, culture fears passion. It fears the loss of control over one's instinctual need for love and deep feelings, just as the ancient Hebrews—specifically men—feared having more facility with sensuality than women. We both desire and fear sensual pleasure. The ambivalent nature of men's dealing with women and sexual pleasure has pushed them to a power-over relationship with the women they love and fear.

As Michel Foucault points out in *The History of Sexuality*, the regulation of aphrodisia, or sensual pleasure, by the ancient Greeks was considered essential to an individual's health and well-being.[5] Of course, as James Miller mentions in the Passion of Micel Foucault, Foucault was determined to develop a thesis that was consistent with his opposition to any kind of law regulating sexual behavior. The ancient Greeks were driven by Daimon, a power or force that drove a person forward. Foucault intended to support a view of the condition in which one's own happiness was controlled by the self. He understood that Christian thinkers brought a sense of malignancy to the full expression of self. Thus, it seems from this perspective that ideas of sexual conduct were proscribed for reasons other than what was good and natural to the human condition.[6]

Additionally, in an article for *The American Historical Review*, Ruth Mazo Karras 2002explains that most historians agree the ancient Greeks were more concerned with "gender roles—masculine or feminine, active or passive—than object choice." There appeared to have been much more freedom in ancient times to practice homosexuality—or, for that matter, practice any sexual preference—than there is today.[7] So where did the construction of the idea that a person should submit to rules that require one sexual partner begin? Where did the idea of sexual conduct and evil become a dominant cultural concern? Let's return for a moment to Reb Nachman's construction of the idea that a holy person such as David couldn't have sinned. Would an extension of this, then, be that God wouldn't have created a world with such a large sexual menu without believing this was good and appropriate? Might Nachman have concluded that God desires man to have sexual freedom?

Certain figures reappear throughout one's exploration of the ideas that have dominated our culture. One of these figures is Saint Augustine of Hippo, who was born in North Africa in 354 AD. Though born into a family that practiced paganism, Augustine ultimately converted to his mother's religion of Catholicism. During his youth, however, he apparently led a hedonistic lifestyle, including maintaining a relationship with a female concubine with whom he had a son. Later in his life, Augustine's mother arranged for him to marry another "more appropriate woman." But while Augustine waited for his fiancée to come of age, he took up with yet another woman. It was during this period that he was said to have written the prayer "Grant me chastity and continence but not yet."[8]

The story then becomes extremely interesting and important. In the summer of 386, at age thirty-two, Augustine went through a spiritual crisis. He read the account of the life of Saint Anthony and converted to Catholicism. He then devoted himself totally to the service of God and practiced celibacy. At this point, he essentially authored the rules and codes of proper sexual conduct, which were practiced in our culture for the next 1,600 years. This man, who seemingly had difficulty with moderating his own sexual passions, professed a way of being that was either-or in structure. In addition, he wrote a theory of dealing with sexual practice that was apparently based on his own lived experience. Saint Augustine had strong words for those who would behave in life as he had:

The union of male and female for the purpose of procreation is the natural good of marriage. But he makes a bad use of this Good who uses it bestially, so that his intention is on the gratification of lust, intend of the desire of offspring . . . fu like manner, therefore, the marriage of believers converts to the use of righteousness that carnal concupiscence. By which "the flesh lusteth against the Spirit." For they entertain the firm purpose of generating offspring to be regenerated—that the children who are born of them as "children of the world" may be born again become "sons of God." Wherefore all parents who do not beget children with this intention, this will this purpose, of transferring them from bring members of the first man into being members of Christ, but boast as unbelieving parents over unbelieving children—however circumspect they be in their cohabitation, studiously limiting it to the begetting of children—really have no conjugal chastity in themselves. For inasmuch as chastity is a virtue, hating chastity as its contrary vice, and as all the virtues (even those whose operations by means of the body) have their seat in the soul, how can the body be in any true sense said to be chaste, when the soul itself is committing fornication against the true God. . . .[9]

Despite the protests of Saint Augustine, it seems that men are not naturally monogamous. In fact, men have apparently been promiscuous for a long time. Michael Hammer, a researcher at the University of Arizona, found that far fewer men than women pass on their genes to subsequent generations. He discovered this after studying the mitochondrial DNA (which follows the female line) and Y-chromosome DNA (which follows the male line) in three discrete populations: the Khoisan of southern Africa, the Khalkha of Mongolia, and the highlanders of Papua New Guinea. In addition, he found that there is a lot of variability in the female DNA and much in the male DNA.[10]

According to Hammer's research, fewer men in each of these three groups contributed their DNA to the gene pool than the women did. In other words, half as many men over the years as women have passed on their genes. Thus, since it takes one man and one woman to create a child, it seems that half as many men in these groups have procreated with twice as many women. Perhaps, then, the rules of sexual conduct promulgated by Saint Augustine and other Christians are working against the natural instincts of the human species. Furthermore, the abundant use of pornography on the Internet may arguably be the healthy strivings of an increasingly frustrated species.

That being said, it is not my intention to suggest that any expression of sexual desire is good or appropriate. The same values that have guided this postmodern discussion apply here as well. Evil develops in situations that are laden with binary thinking, lack of appropriate information, simplistic solutions to complex situations, and power over behavior. The act of rape clearly meets the standard for evildoing. By definition, rape always includes an unwilling victim of aggression. This victim is marginalized by the rapist and seen as a sexual object, not a person. The rapist mostly uses poorly thought-out rationalizations to explain their poor behavior. Furthermore, the act of rape often has more to do with narratives of weakness and inferiority than with enacting sexual pleasure.

In reviewing the acts of King David—or, for that matter, former president Clinton—you may have noticed the possibility of these acts being defined as evil based on the paradigms outlined earlier in this book. In both instances, it wasn't the act of desiring a beautiful woman and engaging in sexual pleasure with her that was the source of evil. Nor was it even the fact that both men wanted to participate in sexual acts outside their primary relationships. The possible evil in these situations comes largely from each leader's abuse of power. In King David's instance, he didn't own up to his desire for Bathsheba. So rather than being forthright and dealing with the choices he and his lover made, he withheld information from Uriah (and other people) and used subterfuge to try to cover up his impropriety. Ultimately, he took advantage of his position and had Uriah killed. Similarly, Clinton had sexual relations with an intern, a woman who was beholden to him. Thus, an unfair power differential already existed between these individuals. And much like King David, Clinton lied and attempted to distort the public's understanding of his poor behavior.

Every day. psychologists like myself witness the evil acts of others as part of our clinical practice. Oftentimes the theme of sexual perversity obscures the actual basis for evil. Unfortunately, the culture's dominant concern is related to the themes around sexual expression. These themes direct us away from behavior that is controlling and objectifying. Thus, we find ourselves embroiled in discussions around possible sexual perversity instead of pursuing narratives that may be at the heart of the problems of those who seek our assistance.

Recently, a couple came to me for therapy. The husband and wife had been married for less than a year and had been struggling for some time. The wife's expressed concern was that her husband was sexually perverse. She began her narrative by saying, "One night, I surprised him and unexpectedly came home from work. I found him in bed, masturbating. Worse yet, he was wearing ladies' underwear." The husband was clearly mortified that he had been caught by her and appeared embarrassed as the wife went on, weeping. "What am I to do?" she said at one point. "I obviously didn't know him when I married him. I don't think that I can live another day with him."

I asked the wife if other issues or concerns had cropped up since the couple had started living together. She said that, for the most part, things were okay, other than his "disgusting secret life." Then I asked the husband what he hoped to accomplish in therapy. He was quite contrite: "Obviously, there's something wrong with me. I know that it's odd that I get off by wearing women's underwear, but it really excites me."

I asked him if he knew whether other men behaved this way. He said that he never had heard of such behavior. I told him that it actually wasn't all that unusual. What I was mostly curious about was whether he would prefer this to having sex with his wife. He said that he had resumed masturbating after months of them not consummating their marriage.

Surprised, I asked the couple, "Have you talked with each other about the lack of sexual relations in your marriage?"

The husband quickly replied, "She is very shy and private."

The wife responded, "I obviously intuited how perverse he is."

Despite the original presentation—that the husband was perverse, which both husband and wife agreed on—it quickly became apparent that the couple lacked a foundation of collaborative dialogue in their relationship. As a result, there was no quality of intimacy in their marriage. The husband, rather than being defined as perverse, was a kind, gentle man who was fearful of being aggressive toward his wife. The wife, on the other hand, was extremely powerful and controlling, and was having difficulty hearing her husband's needs and concerns. Mercifully, the marriage ended after ten sessions of therapy.

Chapter Eleven: What Is Thinking?

A discussion of evil wouldn't be complete without addressing the problem of thinking. What is a thought? Where is it located? What are the origins of our thoughts? Attempting to contemplate the nature of a thought can be disconcerting. Frequently, our attempts at comprehending thought take on a mystical quality. For instance, as you've been reading this book, what ideas have been stimulated? Had you previously imagined that these thoughts may reside in your consciousness? Why was one thought or another triggered by certain stimuli? It should be clear by this point that thoughts are born out of dialogue. This dialogue begins long before our consciousness, and even before our birth. Philosophers often refer to the term *qualia* as the introspectively accessible qualities of our mental lives. Whatever the exact nature of this mind phenomenon, the process of thinking requires a dialectic process between our biological being, our cultural and historical past, our present or contemporary interrelations, and our internal lexicon.

Harlene Anderson, PhD, and Harold A. Goolishian, PhD, wrote one of the most important papers in psychotherapy, which was published in *Family Process* in 1988. In this paper on human systems as linguistic systems, they proposed that human systems are language-generating and, simultaneously, meaning-making systems and that meaning and understanding are socially and intersubjectively constructed.[1] In other words, from birth onward, humans are always trying to make sense of things. We are constantly integrating perceptions and stimuli through our sensorium into our understanding of the world.

In 1990, Jerome Bruner, among others, suggested that from an early age, children organize their experiences as a narrative. According to Bruner, children listen to stories, then integrate them into their experiences and, ultimately, tell these stories. He also distinguishes the necessary characteristics of narratives as "(a) being sequential: composed of a unique series of events, mental states . . . that do not . . . have a life or meaning of their own; except in a narrative structure; and (b) are factually indifferent and can be real or imaginary, having a structure that is internal to the discourse."[2] Thus, the stories children learn and tell have an aspect to them that are experienced as real and true. Whether those stories are about the three blind mice, Santa Claus, or the boogeyman, children live their lives as though these stories are true.

The thought that we love Grandma or that Dad is the smartest man in the world comes from a similar construction. There is a need on the part of the family or community to teach an idea that becomes embedded in the narrative. A familiar phrase in most families is "I love you." This sentence is repeated over and over to a child as they grow toward maturity. By the time the child reaches the age of approximately two to two and a half years old, they are repeating these words. However, what does this phrase mean to the child? Does "I love you" mean the same thing from one family to another? By the time a child is in school, the teacher is reinforcing this idea to the class. Most of the children in the class, therefore, accept this idea and probably think that love in their life has a similar meaning to love in their classmates' lives.

In May 2006, the story of Warren Jeffs and his followers received a lot of attention. Jeffs is still considered to be the leader of the Fundamentalist Church of Jesus Christ of Latter-Day Saints even though the FBI arrested him that year for practicing polygamy. According to an article written by John Doughtery for *Phoenix New Times*, "Jeffs and his band of hard-core polygamists are providing the public with chilling insight into the abuses of the practice, the most alarming of which is the sexual predation of underage girls."[3] One might imagine that a child who was brought up within the tradition of Jeffs's cult would have an entirely different understanding of the meaning behind the phrase "I love you" from a child who was brought up in more traditional Christian families. Clearly, the meaning of words depends on the history and context of the lives of the individuals who are engaged in any one instance of meaning-making.

Recently, one of my clients spoke with me about how, even though his family and friends considered him to be successful, he felt as though he had never fully attained his level of capability. Despite attending several major colleges (including Harvard) in the past, he had only become a senior product manager. When I pointed out that he was also an instructor at the local community college, he responded by diminishing his accomplishment: "I went to some of the most prestigious colleges in the country, have two master's degrees, and I teach at a community college. Wouldn't you think I might be doing something better?"

After some thought, I said, "You have spent a great deal of time and energy studying the Polish culture. You are an Eastern European scholar. You travel regularly to Poland and are a fan and close follower of Eddie Van Halen. You smoke cigars and drink fine brandy. Isn't that success?"

My client looked at me and said, "Why do you think that causes me to be so melancholy? Why can't I fully appreciate my choices? I feel caught between the world that I have created and the world that I perceive others defining as correct and meaningful."

"What were your goals?" I asked. "Did you want to be a part of the Protestant culture?"

"Shit no! I never wanted to join the Anglicans as my brother did. I am a Pole. I won't allow myself to be co-opted."

"So is melancholia a part of being Polish? Or is moving to a higher level the imperative that guides you?"

He stared back at me and said, "Wow. I never realized how much the story of the Polish people has guided my trip. I wanted to defeat the Protestants, not join them. Maybe I should start enjoying the character I've created."

Culture has a major role in determining and shaping our thoughts. The ideas, beliefs, and language of our predecessors are a major part of what shapes our thinking and experiences. As with my client, much of this shaping is done without the individual's conscious awareness. Over the history of humanity, we have developed mechanisms for understanding and integrating the world around us. This is not a mystical process; rather, it is dictated to us by our genetic inheritance and predisposition. How we understand this information is determined and directed by the cultural context we are born into.

The human experience is clearly interactive between our biological capacities and the social environment. Researchers have stressed that biochemical and neurophysiological mechanisms, though involved in brain functioning, are insufficient in explaining the complexities of learning:

We do not inherit culture biologically. We inherit genes which make us capable of acquiring culture by training, learning, imitation of our parents, playmates, teachers, newspapers books, advertisements, propaganda, plus our own choices, decisions and the productions of reflection and speculation. Our genes enable us to learn and to deliberate. What we learn comes not from the genes but from associations, direct and indirect with other men.[4]

A child has the capacity to observe and learn from the world. Just as important, however, is their capability to organize mechanisms internally through language and narratives, which are approximate replications of the language and stories used by the people around them. This is not a simple occurrence by any means. It does not appear to be imitation learning or mimicry. Rather, through observing and participating in their world, the child absorbs a host of factors, including their interactions with their parent(s), other siblings, and the world in general.

An individual's relationship with their world is constantly adapting. Humans are engaged in an evolutionary process of assimilating new information and accommodating themselves to new material. In his book *The Protean Self*, Robert Jay Lifton explains that the contemporary world's requirements for a person include having the capacity for a protean self. He recognizes that for an individual to survive in a world of "multiplicity and polyvocality," the individual must have the capability for continued growth and adaptation throughout their life.[5]

According to Lifton, the development of self has at least three manifestations:

It is sequential.

It has the capacity for multiplicity (i.e., it has the capacity for varied and even antithetical images at the same time).

It is social and takes on forms and variations that are necessary for operation in multiple contexts.[6]

An individual is immersed in a complex matrix that requires continual re-understanding and renegotiation of not only meaning but also identification. To the degree that individuals in today's society become immersed in one particular worldview or another, they may be unprepared to contend with the contingencies and demands of an increasingly complicated world. Negotiating our world requires being capable of flexibility and openness to new meaning-making. An individual's negotiation of meaning takes place within a multiplex created by the convergence of their biological entity, including stages of ontological development and genetic capacity; the individual's historical and cultural past; and their ongoing conversation with a significant other. Each conversation brings the possibility for new and multiple meanings. Within this schema, objectivity or objective reality has no basis. The world is created and recreated by the nature of the participants in any relationship. A system composed of two or more individuals has the possibility of developing ideas or explanations that are new and creative. A person's world is in continuous evolution. To the degree that an individual has the capacity for flexible and creative negotiations between themselves and others, they would be considered nonproblematic or healthy.

Let's use diagram 1 below to visualize this idea at the intersection point of the three axes of thought: biological, cultural/linguistic, and dialogic (e.g., between you and others)

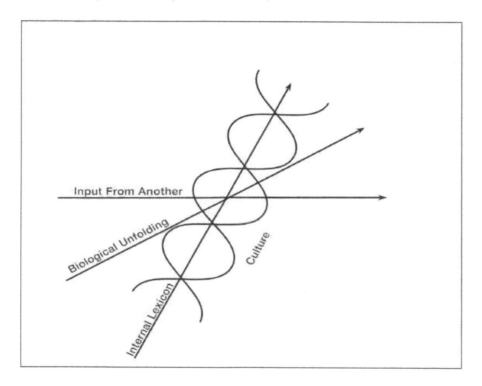

Diagram 1: [Interenal dialogue]

The first axis represents a person's biological or physiological development as well as their ontological unfolding. Obviously, a child has a different capacity for understanding information at different times in their development. A one-year-old, before developing language skills, incorporates information differently than an older child with language does. A sixteen-year-old has developed an even greater capacity for sophisticated thinking.

The second axis represents a person's internal lexicon. This axis can be understood as a double helix of culture or history and language. The unfolding child incorporates previously formed ideas from other individuals or sources that become the child's lenses for interpreting new stimuli. As noted earlier in this chapter, to the degree an individual has the capacity for multiplicity and polyvocality, they can also participate in creative dialogue. Several strands form the makeup of the internal helix of the person's lexicon. Many voices, ideas, and even conflicting thoughts exist within the construction of the self.

The third axis represents the input from another person(s) in the conversation. This can also represent the input an individual receives from their culture through books, movies, or the media. To the degree a person has developed a level of internal comfort and equanimity is the degree to which they can receive new or unique information—or, for that matter, the degree to which they accept their own internal dissonance (e.g., accepting the multiplicity of ideas and voices within the self, having the capacity to receive dissonant ideas).

Conversations can take place externally and internally. We are all aware that while we are involved in a conversation with another person, that person is engaged in a similar process with us. They are forming their thoughts at a similar point of intersection within themselves. The conversation then produces an expanded opportunity for newness. Though paradigm shifts or truly original thinking or ideas are rare, a conversation can bring about creative thinking. The expanded lexicon created by the inclusion of others always produces new possibilities.

Diagram 2 below was adapted from a picture drawn by Tom Anderson, MD, in 2005 when he was visiting my practice:

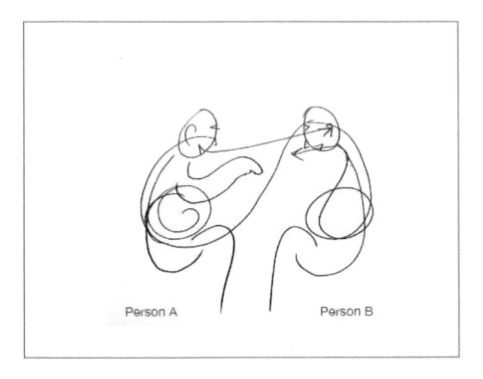

Person A   Person B

Diagram 2: [Reflexive Conversation]

Similarly, dialogues take place within us. Many voices and views are incorporated into our being. These views, thoughts, ideas, memories, and philosophies exist within us simultaneously. In other words, these voices are in dialogue with one another. Harry S. Sullivan, in his book *The Interpersonal Theory of Psychiatry*, takes elaborate pains to describe a process he calls *personification*. He recognizes that the external world, through dialogic relationships, was incorporated into a person's internal world. In this process, a child's dyadic relationships in particular are incorporated into a self-system made of a good self and a bad self.[7] Though this can be a useful metaphor, it is limiting in its structure. As our conversations continue throughout our life, they are always open to change and renegotiation. These internal conversations are available for rethinking and new possibilities.

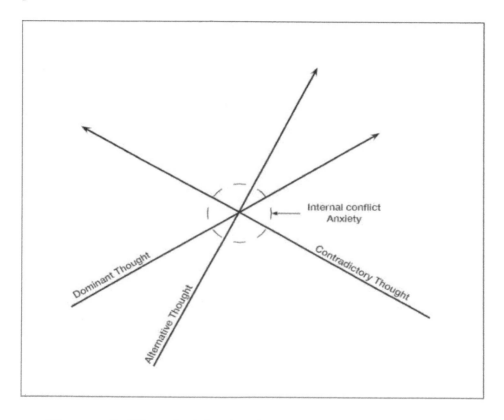

Diagram 3: [Thought Stimulated Externally]

If we look into ourselves, we will realize that thoughts emerge without another person there for a conversation. One idea or another may emerge, and we begin an internal process of evaluating the construction of that idea. For instance, let's take the question, "Tell me about a significant person in your life, such as your mother." This question can evoke many possible ideas or thoughts. Is the person you conjure up your mother today? Or is it a version of her from a previous time in your life, such as your adolescence or childhood? All these images and voices coexist within the mind and inform us during internal or external conversations.

Just as several memories or images inform us during our thoughts, so do ideas and philosophies. Let's say that an individual is asked a complex question such as "Do you believe in God and religion? And does that preclude a belief in evolution?" The individual may respond by saying that both belief systems can coexist in their head; one is possibly based on their faith, and the other possibly based on science and evidence. A healthy person can balance thoughts and ideas without anxiety. They don't have to eliminate a possibility because it has aspects that are contradictory to other important thoughts or beliefs.

It is possible to be angry about an individual's behavior yet understand their actions. We can be loyal supporters of a government yet disagree with aspects of its policies. The internal dialogue of a nonproblematic individual is flexible and open. Multiple possibilities can exist simultaneously. Some of these possibilities may be contradictory or even paradoxical. Many recent discoveries in science and technology would be off-putting if not for our capacity to tolerate ambiguity and paradox.

The rules that apply to an evaluation of evil that is external to an individual also apply to the process within an individual's internal dialogue. The more that one voice or another dominates the internal conversation, the less likely it is for reasonable outcomes to occur. A person's internal dialogue can become ossified or rigid. This may happen as a result of a particular philosophy or code dominating the individual's internal conversation or the individual incorporating voices that reject potential creative ideas. Much like a virus, certain deeply held beliefs prevent new or interesting material from being incorporated into a person's internal conversation. For example, continuously reinforced opinions from one's parents can produce responses in a child that flood them with anxiety and prevent them from incorporating new possibilities. One such statement is, "You will go to hell if you don't practice our faith!"

The rule of binary thinking directly applies to an individual's internal dialogues. For instance, the internal dialogue of "us versus them" is experienced as "me and not me." During therapy sessions, clients frequently tell me that they have ideas they experience as alien.

These ideas are troublesome to them because they are inconsistent with the client's dominant idea or story. These ideas are often talked about as "not me." Due to the disturbing nature of these ideas, they go undiscussed by the client outside of therapy. The individual frequently denies those ideas in discussions with friends and family and often projects them onto others. So rather than being claimed by the individual as "a part of me," these ideas squirrel about inside the individual's head, becoming the source of increased anxiety and consternation.

Dominating thoughts and belief systems often are the source of experiencing an idea as "not me." The more rigid and intolerant the dominating system, the greater the likelihood of experiencing a thought as alien or "not me." Unsurprisingly, many of the most fundamental thinkers have behaved hypocritically. An example of this comes from Mark Foley, a former Republican representative from Florida. While Foley was writing laws to prevent sexual exploitation on the Internet, he was sexually exploiting pages in Congress. It must be assumed that Foley was incapable of discussing and exploring his sexual feelings.

In all probability, aspects of Foley's internal conversations were conflicting with the dominant beliefs he had been taught. From childhood onward, he might have avoided discussing the thoughts and feelings emerging within him that were opposite to the teachings he received from other people. He probably couldn't accept his internal dialogues regarding sexual interests, so he worked hard at denying them. The eventual result was an individual who attempted to portray himself as something he was not while simultaneously living a secret life.

Frequently, clients reveal to me secret ideas they find to be shameful. These ideas are inconsistent with the dominant belief systems they have incorporated into their lives, and they run the complete gamut of ideas and behavior that are discouraged in society's dominant conversations. Some clients have said that they were attracted to their best friend's wife. Others admitted to participating in clandestine meetings on the Internet. Still others confessed to fantasizing about sex with children or to secretly eating or drinking while claiming to be on a diet. In almost all of these instances, the clients who reported these shameful thoughts and acts also experienced those thoughts and acts as "not me."

Obviously, individuals who can't tolerate aspects of their internal dialogues also keep these thoughts secret. As with the discussion of evil in society, this control of internal dialogues and information leads to secretive functioning. Secrets invariably lead an individual into problematic situations. One of the most common problematic situations that has arisen during my therapy sessions is when one partner in a marriage finds that their sex life is no longer satisfying.

Often, the individual is fearful of sharing this thought with their spouse. They are concerned that their partner will become hurt or angry and thus further retreat from the relationship. Instead of sharing these thoughts honestly and clearly, many people look for new outlets for their sexual feelings. This lack of honest, open communication often leads the individual—and, ultimately, the marriage—into trouble.

For some individuals, it is an even greater problem when they can't tolerate their own experience of parts of their internal dialogue. These individuals, in essence, don't allow themselves to think their own thoughts. This level of control of internal information is consistent with extremely primitive functioning. The thoughts are so shameful to the individual that they often deny the thoughts' existence. This problem eventually leads the individual to behave as though they have no rationale for their behavior. A person may find their own thoughts so repulsive that they can't bear to think them. As with former Congressman Foley, such individuals often project these thoughts into the world, where they can tolerate and ultimately control those thoughts better.

At times, people may find their internal dialogue so intolerable that they experience the entire dialogue as "not me." When an individual perceives large parts of their internal dialogue as noxious or considers a portion of their dialogue to be reprehensible, they may experience dissociation. Such individuals obviously can't think in clear and constructive ways.

As individuals lose their capacity to be in touch with the different components of themselves, they become increasingly limited in their capability to plan, think, and strategize. Thus, the less often they bring in new and alternative points of view, the more likely they are to develop stylized and parochial solutions to problems. Their inner life then becomes dominated by a particular philosophy or bias, and possibilities for creative thinking become increasingly limited. This leads us back to one of the basic tenets of evil discussed earlier in this book: finding simplistic solutions to complex problems. Individuals are more likely to participate in generating simplistic solutions when their internal life does not have the fluidity and flexibility to balance new information with older beliefs.

A healthy individual can orient themself to the contingencies and requirements of the world around them. They can freely examine the multiplicity of alternatives in their life space. They are not overwhelmed by events or ideas that are inconsistent with their dominant belief systems. Nor do they fear new ideas or possibilities. In other words, they are adaptable.

A problematic individual, however, is rigid and can't contemplate alternatives. Their behavior seems almost conditioned. Particular situations are almost certain to evoke predictable responses from them. So rather than effectively assessing new events, this individual imposes ideas from their long-held belief systems onto the world. They invoke old solutions to problems even when those solutions haven't succeeded. Their thinking is simplistic and incomplete, and they maintain their belief systems over solving complex problems.

As we have examined the internal development of an individual's thoughts, the idea that certain deeply held beliefs and philosophies can hold sway over newer ideas and thoughts keeps emerging. We have all experienced the anxiety associated with challenging the ideas we have lived by and taken for granted. And as discussed throughout this book, our culture—mainly through the institutions of family, school, and religion—have ingrained and reinforced dominating ideas within us. These ideas resist the incorporation of beliefs that challenge them. Guilt and shame are the experiences of power over behavior in one's internal dialogue. And as these anxious feelings intensify, we become less effective in our capacity to participate in external conversations. We have difficulty with thinking through problems and become more susceptible to doing hurtful things to others. After all, doing damage to others is often born out of the fear that they will harm us.

Chapter Twelve: The Other

Obviously, a discussion of evil requires some thought around the position of "the other." In the common parlance of psychotherapists, the other is often referred to as the identified patient, or IP. Throughout this book, I have shared case studies demonstrating how limited modern psychotherapeutic practice remains in its approach to the IP. My practice in Salem, Massachusetts, has been built largely around very difficult cases. Time and time again, my colleagues and I are referred individuals who are thought to have major psychiatric illness but, in actuality, are often the healthiest members of their family.

Family systems theory demonstrated long ago that the IP serves a useful purpose for the family. The IP serves a role in either homeostasis (i.e., maintaining the family's current status) or morphogenesis (i.e., pushing the family to a higher level of functioning). According to Margoroh Maruyama, any living system depends on these two self-sustaining processes. The system must maintain itself in light of environmental vagaries.[1]

But what is the experience of the other? Or, rather, what is the experience of the IP? If these individuals are healthy, why do they allow themselves to be subjected to the stress and abuse that this role often necessitates? Furthermore, what is it about societal practices that require the identification of certain individuals to fall outside the norm? Can a group or society function well without outsiders, or without identifying certain persons or groups as the other?

When considering the second question, two concepts from the family therapy movement—pseudomutuality and pseudohostility—come to mind. *Pseudomutuality* is seen every day in clubs, fraternities, and most other social organizations in our culture. If we look the same—possibly by wearing the same clothes, acting the same, or watching the same television shows and movies—then we are the same. We are part of the "in group" and hopefully free from the scrutiny or abuse that is heaped upon "the other." But in reality, we may think or feel differently from other members of the group. Our outward public presentation nevertheless gives off this signal: "I am one of you. If I wear the same varsity sweater you're wearing or the club's blue blazer, the message I'm sending is that I am okay and please leave me alone."

Throughout the different levels of social organization within a community, several examples exist that show a demand upon the community to perform in pseudomutuality. Until recently, the official policy of the United States Armed Forces regarding homosexuality was "Don't ask, don't tell." In other words, if a uniformed soldier looked, dressed, and acted like a heterosexual individual, their private life wasn't scrutinized. However, if they blatantly expressed a sexual preference other than the one prescribed by the dominant discourse of the US Armed Services, they were dismissed from military service. Despite overwhelming evidence that members of the LGBTQ community have performed meritoriously while in service, the dominant culture didn't allow their sexual preferences to be explored openly.

This phenomenon has also been in place in other sectors of the community. From time to time, professional athletes are thought by the public to identify as something other than heterosexual. Male athletes in particular must be scrupulous in maintaining any secrets about this aspect of their lives. It matters little to society that the athlete is a great quarterback or diver. They still become suspect in their capacity to perform and are carefully scrutinized.

Let's also look back on President George W. Bush's dictum, "You're either with me or you're against me."[2] Isn't this a demand from the then-president for all of us to get in line with his policies? In a not-so-veiled manner, he accused those who openly disagreed with him of being disloyal to the government. The implementation of the Patriot Act by Congress in2001en legitimized the president's threat against those individuals. People within our communities, especially those of the Islamic faith, are now in danger of being accused of treason if they support groups and policies that oppose the stated policies of the US government.

At every level of community politics, we are reminded not to be too discordant from cultural imperatives. Some people warn us of the consequences of speech that is too strident. Others would have us criminalize flag burning. Still others call the American Civil Liberties Union *pinkos* because they represent the right of "the other" to speak their mind. My students have frequently reminded me that, because I teach at a state college, I have to be careful about how I express my ideas. From junior high onward, we have been immersed in a world of pseudomutual demands. From the time a child learns the consequences of wearing the wrong jeans to school, they have experienced the consequences of ignoring pseudomutual thinking. And by the time we grow into the role of citizen, we have each had much experience with the demands of pseudomutuality upon our expression of ideas.

Pseudohostility is also an experience that we all know well. In this instance, the group coheirs around scapegoating a particular victim. Pseudohostility is seen every day in every high school cafeteria in our culture. A student is marked as a target, even though they have done nothing ostensibly wrong. However, they are identified as "the other" for some noticeable difference such as a birthmark, a mole, or their physical stature. Some students are excluded for being too tall or too short. Others are tormented for wearing the "wrong clothes" or not honoring a group's informal hierarchy. The reality is that these individuals—teenage students, in this case—are designated to be "the other" for no meaningful reason.

This observation is consistent with the thinking of French sociologist Émile Durkheim. He concluded that deviance has several societal functions, including the following:

Affirmation of cultural values and norms

Clarifying moral boundaries

Promoting social unity

Encouraging social change[3]

In other words, there is nothing necessarily wrong with the behavior of the deviant, or "the other." Deviations come from the formation of norms and values that the group chooses to enforce. The group then arbitrarily institutes rules for maintaining this system.

When students are interviewed about their hurtful or taunting attitudes toward a victim, they often report great remorse for their behavior. However, they also report the belief that not participating in the scapegoating—or, even worse, ridiculing such behavior—could result in their own victimization. Joining in the scapegoating of "the other" seems to provide safety for the perpetrators while solidifying the group's boundaries. Once again, throughout different levels within society, we witness pseudohostile behavior. Are we witnessing basic mechanism by which groups need to form and maintain themselves? Or are we watching an artifact of the teachings of our culture?

As demonstrated throughout this book, evil appears to be a relative matter. It is not determined by a set of concrete propositions that are inherent to the conduct of social organizations. In fact, evil is not what it appears to be. In the high school example, the group's arbitrary victim is portrayed as the evil party. However, it is the group's behavior that demonstrates the characteristics of evil.

In both pseudomutuality and pseudohostility, we see the four factors that lead to the construction of evil. The first factor, binary thinking, clearly exists in both situations. The group chooses a victim ("the other") and determines that the individual is at odds with them. Second, no one in the group is allowed to share their opposition to the hurtful behavior (control of information). Questioning the group's actions is also considered unacceptable. Third, the group solves the questions of its membership and boundaries in a simplistic, destructive manner (simple solutions to complex problems). Finally, the use of power over behavior is rampant in both scenarios. The victim is continuously taunted and bullied. Ultimately, the group's tyranny allows these mechanisms to operate.

When observing such poor behavior from high school students, we are forced to contemplate the possible cultural antecedents of these behaviors. Looking back at the origins of Judeo-Christian culture, we are reminded of the story of Chanukah. In 168 BC, many people from the privileged class of Jews sought the advantages of the Hellenistic Society. By giving up the traditions and mores of their birth group, they could gain access to the Greeks' material and cultural benefits.

The Jewish labor class, however, demonized assimilation with the Greeks. They joined with the priests and vilified the culture of Plato, Aristotle, and Sophocles. Mattathias, a Jewish priest and leader, became incensed with the conduct of an apostate Jew who had bowed down before the Greek gods. So Mattathias killed him, and a rebellion against the Greek king Antiochus followed. Depending on an individual's perspective, Chanukah can be viewed as a holiday celebrating the rights of individuals to practice the religion of their choice or as a holiday celebrating the maintenance of the rules of the group (in this case, the Jews). It gives license to the destruction of those who wish to practice in ways that are "other."

Furthermore, within ten to twenty years of the events described above, a group known as the Essenes, an extremely pious and celibate sect, referred to all Jews who were willing to participate in more universal practices as apostate. They accused such people of having been seduced by the power of evil. Again, who is evil and who is "the other" depends on an individual's perspective.

In this example, the pious Jews are referring to those who practiced the Greeks' cultural practices as evil. However, just as the Jews contributed to the development of Western values, so did the Greeks. Today, neither of these great peoples are considered to be evil. Yet both cultures demeaned each other's values and practices. In this cultural and historical context, we can begin to appreciate that "the other" can be—or is—us.

Similarly, the Persians saw the Greeks as the children of the lie. The Greeks saw the Jews as uncultured and attempted to assimilate them into their ways, while the Jews saw both groups as unclean and evil. Just as with the high school students, each group seems to reinforce its rules and boundaries by diminishing those they identify as different.

Likewise, in the daily practice of psychotherapy, a counselor is exposed to the pain and consternation of their IPs, or (as defined earlier in this chapter) "the other." This experience can take on many different forms. Frequently, the IP is perplexed as to why they have been excluded from or victimized by the dominant group. That group could be their peers at school or their family. Oftentimes, the IP becomes angry over being treated poorly for no apparent reason—or, for that matter, being treated poorly due to a particular attribute or belief. This fear of being excluded or marginalized by a group often motivates us to participate in hurtful practices. Individuals seemingly need to be included in the community's dominant discourse. Thus, they are willing to ignore their own needs to receive the positive regard of those they deem to be important.

In 1964, Carl Rogers noted that the need for parental regard superseded a child's natural inclinations. This striving toward pleasing one's parents, even at the risk of never truly satisfying one's natural drives toward love and curiosity, is extended to the social group and the community at large. So desperately do we seek the love of others that we are willing to abandon our authentic selves and our values. Our fear and anxiety over being excluded drive us to participate in and identify with a group's pseudomutual or pseudohostile behaviors. The experience of being "the other" is the force that leads us to treat other people in these hurtful ways. Ironically, our own experience of being the same as "the other" leads to us behaving badly. Just as with the Jews, the Greeks, and the Persians, the illusion keeps us separated.

Currently, we are living in a tribal society where the things that separate us outweigh the traits that unite us. Unfortunately, Donald Trump continues to emphasize society's divides. Even though he is no longer in office, he spins falsehoods that scare approximately a third of the US population. These include statements such as "The election was stolen from the people," "Those who are in power are socialists, who will take away individual rights," and "Black and

Brown immigrants don't hold our values." How else can we understand otherwise reasonable people who are espousing the bizarre notions of QAnon? Even for some Republicans, it is as though they can't be accepted as genuine fundamentalists of their party unless they accept Trump's ideas.

Trump's successor as US president, Democrat Joe Biden, is trying to emphasize unity but has not succeeded in his messaging. Even his own party is fractured. There seems to be little understanding of dialogue and collaboration. We have made one another the problem rather than emphasizing the problems that exist currently in society, such as climate change, infrastructure, disease, and healthcare. If Democrats can't come together to discuss solutions to today's problems, the communities of the United States will once again be facing the development of evil.

Chapter Thirteen: Puck the Jester, or Bill Maher

Confronting evil often requires getting the community's attention. However, those who are in power often can't or are unwilling to participate in responsible dialogue and explore the consequences of their culture's practices. These individuals are frequently too ingrained in the situation to allow for a successful exploration of the issues. And all too often, the people who are responsible for challenging the dominant discourse of those in charge lack the courage to criticize them. Who, then, in any given culture is responsible for challenging powerful men who are behaving poorly?

Throughout recent history, we have seen examples of subordinates capitulating to the inexcusable behavior of their superiors. How easily it appears to be for low-level managers in our businesses and government to follow the poorly thought-out prescriptions of their leadership. Whether it is out of fear of the power brokers, or out of a hope to become part of the power establishment, we observe time and time again the young, inexperienced neophyte's reluctance to challenge authority.

How else could Kenneth Lay have eviscerated his company, Enron, and its employees? Additionally, during the Trump administration, we witnessed the obsequious behaviors of US Attorney General William Barr and Secretary of State Mike Pompeo. These and other individuals refused to dispute the lies and distortion of then-President Donald Trump. Essentially, they each refused to challenge their boss, instead allowing for poor—if not illegal—practices to continue.

Since time immemorial, the court jester has often gotten their king's attention. The jester, through humor and irony, frequently challenges the edicts of the court. Currently in our culture, people like Bill Maher, Jon Stewart, and Whoopi Goldberg bring the truth before the public. It seems that the most powerful form of criticism in our community comes from comedians. They cause the rest of us to face ourselves. They hold up a mirror to those in power and convince the community and its leaders to reflect on public policy.

As a therapist, I have always understood that the IP's role is to bring attention to their family's dysfunctional behavior. Though the IP does not have quite the same role as the court jester, certain aspects of the two are similar. The IP, much like the jester, is responsible for identifying problems within the family system and then amplifying them so that they are clearly visible. In this way, the IP often holds up a mirror to their parents and family so that they can see themselves more clearly.

In my practice, the teenage child is often identified as the patient. Their behavior frequently requires the family to examine their decision-making process and reorganize themselves to better deal with family tensions. Some of the more blatant examples of IP behavior would rank up there with the humorous behavior of Maher or Stewart. In fact, I remember one particular phone call that one of my colleagues received from a frantic mother.

"I was just given your name by the school counselor," the mother said at the beginning of the call. "I don't know what's going on, but my son has been sent home from school. He was suspended. He's never been in trouble. We were told you are very experienced in working with troubled children."

"Please tell me what happened," my colleague responded.

"I think he's lost his mind. He behaved in a way that's uncharacteristic of him." The mother began sobbing at this point. Once she had composed herself, she continued. "My husband and I are so ashamed of his behavior."

"I'm curious," my colleague said. "What did he do?"

"He was supposed to give an oral presentation in his world history class. I don't know . . . He walked to the front of the class, turned his back to them, dropped his pants, and mooned the teacher and his classmates."

After the call, I was asked to be a consultant to my colleague. Initially, I chuckled to myself. Why was this a problem that was causing the boy's mom to worry so much? After all, haven't we all been children? Haven't each of us felt like mooning our teachers and parents before? And like so many other cases I had been involved with, this was a precursor to much more problematic behavior within the family.

As you can probably imagine from the short conversation my colleague had had with the boy's mother, this family was weighed down by generations of expectation and demand. The boy was furious with his parents for projecting on him their need to continue their Ivy League legacy. Shortly after beginning therapy, the issues shifted to the mother and father's problematic relationship.

As I have noted time and time again in this book, the presenting problem is often a marker of other difficulties in the family system. In this case, the adolescent "jester" was responding to the rigid, dogmatic views of his parents. The parents, on the other hand, were not listening to him—or, for that matter, to each other. Thus, the child had demonstrated his need for making room for his own voice in the family.

Humor is an essential ingredient in life. It is not just a tool for confronting evil or poor behavior, but also a vehicle for making life more palatable—a mechanism for relieving the stress and pressure of everyday life. Those of us who work in helping professions recognize the relief we often achieve from the black, macabre humor we share after our sessions. For instance, after a dark, painful meeting with a depressed patient, my intern once said, "What's up with that? What's her problem? She makes me feel like jumping out the window." I quickly responded by telling my intern that if she jumped, I would stick my head out the window afterward and say *plop*. The intern looked at me and said, "How dare you. Don't I mean more to you than *plop*?" The pain we listen to day in and day out often results in us being irreverent and relieving ourselves of the situation with humor.

The origins of the jester's role in our culture go back to ancient times. In Greek mythology, Pan (the god of shepherds and flocks) was thought to have the hind quarters, legs, and horns of a goat, thus resembling a faun or satyr. Though the word *satire* is often mistakenly thought to be derived from the style and behavior of the satyrs who accompanied Pan in the woods, it is actually a style of humorous, ironic play developed by the Romans. The satyrs are believed to be associated with the male sex drive because of their physical similarities to animals. And as noted throughout this book, sex, merriment, and raucous behavior are often associated with evil.

In more recent history, the images of Satan may have been derived from ancient images of Pan. The devil is often depicted as having horns and cloven hooves. Pan, who was the son of Zeus and Hermes, is described in the Homeric epic as having the capacity of "delighting" the gods. Though Pan loved sex and music and was often associated with debauchery, he had the power to inspire sudden fear in people. The word *panic* is derived from his name.

Much like how Pan was often the source of inspiration or fear, the comedians and entertainers of today inspire or create fear in their audience. For instance, during the beginning of an interview between Larry King and Bill Maher on *Larry King Live*, the following banter took place:

King: Tonight, he's back. Bill Maher is back. America's most controversial comic, as outspoken as ever. . . . They either love him or hate him.

Maher: They don't hate me, Larry.

King: Disagree, then, Bill Maher, it's the kids who hate him. Bill Maher is our special guest. He's the host of this week's—

Maher: Actually, kids like me. I don't like them. There's a big difference.

King: I know they like you.

Maher: They do.

King: He's the host—

Maher: They like honesty.[1]

During Shakespearean times, the most famous of Shakespeare's fools was Puck from *A Midsummer Night's Dream*. Puck is a mischievous pre-Christian spirit. Though his actual origins remain unknown, he shares many of the same characteristics as Pan and the satyrs. Oddly enough, in Ireland, the word *puck* is sometimes used as the word for *goat*. In Swedish, Pocker is an old name for the devil; and in Norwegian, a puk is a water sprite, a supernatural being of evil power.

Puck is one of the most important characters in *A Midsummer Night's Dream*. The funny, quick-witted spirit puts many of the play's events into motion. He is an earthy yet delicate fairy, a study in wild contrasts. And much like today's comedians, he uses humor and coarseness to achieve his ends. As the jester of Oberon, King of Fairies, he is both good-hearted and capable of cruel tricks. His responsibility is to illuminate ideas, challenge sensibilities, and possibly offend other characters. As he says at one point in the play, "If we shadows have offended, / Think but this, and all is mended: / That you have but slumbered here, / While these visions did appear."[2]

I once participated in a panel titled "Is Everything Sacred?" at the Newport International Film Festival. It was a fun discussion about the role of humor in society. The panel included several comedians, including *Saturday Night Live* cast members Rachel Dratch and Fred Armisen. As I engaged in this sometimes raucous discussion with the funniest people I had ever met, we discussed topics ranging from Al Franken and the events of 9/11 to censorship in the media. It helped me realize how humor is more important than ever as a mechanism for facing ourselves.

At one point during this panel, the comedians were asked about Federal Communications Commission (FCC) regulations and Howard Stern's radio show. To my surprise, they became strangely quiet. Finally, Fred Armisen mustered up, "The FCC thing with Clear Channel and Howard Stern is really out of line."[3] I came to my panelists' aid afterward:

Longin said he does not agree with the regulations because we as society selectively decide what is useful and what is not useful. For instance, Stern is deemed not useful but Rush Limbaugh is.

Longin said that Stern is more representative of the way people speak.

"I don't get why it's okay to talk like that in real life," Longin said. "Why can't they talk like that on the radio?"

Longin said that people like Stern do a service to the community by offering an outlet to people who could be doing harm. "My problem is that scatological language is a lot less dangerous than guns or bullets," he said. "You need to give people use of language to prevent something bad from happening," Longin said.[4]

Had the shooters at Virginia Tech or Stoneham Douglas High School had words instead of automatic weapons at their disposal, the carnage that took place on both campuses possibly wouldn't have occurred. It always boggles my mind that people become so alarmed at the use of scatological language. Whenever I'm teaching, I remind my students that I often use bawdy language in my class. And from my earliest experiences as a therapist, I have come to understand that using words such as *fuck* or *shit* is much less offensive than using a gun or even a fist.

Besides, it is much less offensive to use graphic language than it is to diminish or demean other people. One of the most important lessons Bill Maher—or, for that matter, George Carlin and Lewis Black—have taught us is that words are often less offensive than the cultural attitudes they expose. Here is one such example from Black:

How to stimulate the economy: Now, what you do is build a big fucking thing. I don't care what it is! As long as it's big and it's a fucking thing! And then the economy will explode, because people would say, "I want to see the Big Fucking Thing!" Then there'll be a Big Fucking Thing restaurant, a Big Fucking Thing hotel and casino, a Big Fucking Thing spa![5]

George Carlin notably took on the FCC in his 1972 monologue "Seven Words You Can Never Say on Television." At the time, the words he used—*shit, piss, fuck, cunt, cocksucker, motherfucker,* and *tits*, presented in that order—were considered inappropriate and unsuitable for television. Then, in 1973, WBAI (an affiliate of the Pacifica radio network) broadcasted a portion of Carlin's album *Occupation: Foole*. The FCC took the station to court. A series of rulings followed this court case that ultimately established indecency regulations in American broadcasting. At a time in American history when thousands of young people were dying in the Vietnam War, the government was fighting with Carlin about the use of "dirty" words.

Carlin's efforts led to the safe harbor provisions of the FCC regulations that grant broadcasters the right to broadcast indecent material between the hours of 10:00 p.m. and 6:00 a.m., when children are presumed to be asleep. Ironically, children are presumed to handle hours of violence and mayhem even though adults fear they will be corrupted by being exposed to words such as *fuck*. Though Carlin never won his court case for the rights of Americans to speak freely, his tenacity and perseverance moved the country to a clear, more sensible policy on the use of language in public.

During a therapy session , one of my clients—a young man in the midst of a critical discussion with his parents—said, "This is fucking outrageous!" His father immediately chimed in, asking his son what he had said. The young man repeated himself: "It is fucking outrageous that you two won't let me stay out with my friends on prom night."

The father's face turned red. "You will not speak like that to your mother and I."

The young man was clearly about to escalate the crisis when I intervened. "Would someone like to explain to me what your goals are right now? Where do you see this conversation going?"

"This is the problem," the father immediately responded. "He has no respect for us. I want him to participate in our family within our rules."

"He's such an asshole," the son retorted. "He always has to be right. He always has to be in control."

I looked directly at the boy and asked, "Do you think that by saying that to your father, you're going to succeed in getting what you want on prom night?"

"Probably not."

"So then what are you doing?"

The boy began laughing, then said, "We're doing what we always do. We're trying to outmuscle each other."

The father nodded. "He's right. I want him to let me be the boss."

I asked the father if he anticipated his son's escalation whenever he made the use of language the issue. "Yes," he responded. "I knew he would be pissed off, but I went there anyway."

185

"Was his language the issue?" I asked. "Was it really where you wanted to go?"

"No," the father said. "It's the kind of distraction that never lets us resolve any issue."

As I reflected on this conversation, I realized that my dad and I would often joust with each other in conversation, much like this father and son were. The difference was that ours never reached the degree of confrontation or assaultiveness that appeared to occur regularly between this dad and his son. What exactly enabled my dad and I to spar safely but led this young man and his father to escalate into mayhem?

Once again, the rules that lead to evildoing can be seen as we compare the two situations. My dad had always shared a caring, loving attitude that superseded the rules that separated and maintained the hierarchy. When rules of decorum or properness supersede the bonds of the relationship, danger can potentially occur. Thus, it appears that love and curiosity are meant to keep us safe.

In society, love, curiosity, and the willingness to provide clear, consistent information are at the heart of us being safe. Unfortunately, today's press is often controlled by those who have special interests in keeping a certain limited perspective in front of us. Even respected newspapers such as *The New York Times* have demonstrated a capacity for being duped by the government.

One example of particularly poor reporting occurred during the campaign conducted by then-US vice president Dick Cheney and his staff to legitimize the US's preemptive attack on Iraq. In the paper's zeal to be a leader of factual information at the start of the Iraq War, *The New York Times* provided misinformation about weapons of mass destruction. Judith Miller, a *Times* reporter, had access to Scooter Libby, Cheney's chief of staff. She believed she was gaining inside information on presidential decision-making, but in reality she was being manipulated to provide the public with misinformation that ultimately outed CIA operative Valerie Plame. However, the greatest consequences of Miller's actions were that she legitimized George W. Bush's administration's position on fighting a war in Iraq. If the process of gaining information about the function of government has been compromised, where can we then learn the truth about government policy and function?

Thus, it seems that our current court jesters have come to our rescue. *The Daily Show*, previously hosted by Jon Stewart, and *Real Time with Bill Maher* (hosted, of course, by Bill Maher) have become the major critics of US government policy. Using humor, their hosts regularly take on the insidious and destructive functions of recent administrations. For instance, during George W. Bush's presidency, Stewart would call attention nightly to the Bush administration's devious practices. He also made this comment when hosting the Peabody Awards in [2006.

Thomas Jefferson once said, "Of course the people don't want war, but the people can be brought to the bidding of their leader. All you have to do is tell them they're being attacked and denounce the pacifists for somehow a lack of patriotism and exposing the country to danger. It works the same in any country." I think that was Jefferson. Oh, wait. That was Hermann Göring. Shoot![6]

However, it is Bill Maher who, in humorous yet intelligent and courageous fashion, is considered the nemesis of the apologists for our dominant cultural themes. Every week, on *Real Time with Bill Maher*, he confronts US cultural and societal practices, including government, religion, language, and the wisdom of our civic leaders. He even risks alienating cultural icons, including presidents and popes In the next section we will review some of Maher's observations on our contemporary society.

Bill Maher on Religion

Maher: Religion, to me, is a bureaucracy between man and God that I don't need. The Bible looks like it started out as a game of Mad Libs.

New rule: *Time Magazine* has to change its name to *God Weekly*. This week, Mary is on the cover again. In the last two years, *Time* has put out [stories like] "The Secrets of the Nativity," "The God Gene," "Faith, God and the Oval Office," "The Bible and the Apocalypse," "Who Was Moses?", "What Jesus Saw," "Why Did Jesus Have to

Die?", "Jesus in 2000." If Jesus gets any more free press, he's going to start thinking he's Paris Hilton. Look, I understand we have a lot of Christians in this nation, but how about a little equal time? "Vishnu to Ganesh: 'Drop Dead'" and "Is There No Pleasing Zeus?"

Caller: Hi. Well, my question is, the Lord spoke to me approximately three years ago, and if the Lord spoke to you [Maher], I was wondering if you'd become a believer.

Maher: No. I'd check into Bellevue, which is what you should do. . . .

Maher: Well, you know, I was raised Catholic.

King: Catholic and Jewish, right?

Maher: Well, I wasn't raised Jewish. My mother is Jewish. But I never even knew I was half-Jewish until I was a teenager. I was just so frightened about the Catholics and everything that was going on there in the [Catholic] Church, and I was never, you know, molested or anything. And I'm a little insulted. 1 guess they never found me attractive. And that's really their loss.

King: You were special, Bill.

Maher: I was very special. You know, I'm just . . . I'm shocked that people are finding out that priests are no altar boys, you know. It's the institution that really needs fixing—and, of course, you really can't fix an institution when it is religion. Because when you say *religion*, immediately you can get away with anything. I mean, look at what the Muslims did with women around the world. If you did that to anybody else, if it wasn't under the guise of religion, you could never get away with stuff like that. . . .[7]

Maher on Bush and the Iraq War

Bill Maher has been a persistent critic of the Iraq war. He has never waivered on his opposition to George Bush's policies and strategies for dealing with the Middle East.

Maher: [*to Richard Perle*] I think you guys might have been right about the big picture. And I'm not above saying, "You know what? Maybe I was wrong." Okay. But on the other half of it, why the incompetence? Why was this war conducted so badly from the beginning? And you have to admit that cost lives. And my theory is because Republicans are sentimentalists, because you guys have such rose-colored glasses about America, that you thought as soon as we showed up in Iraq, they'd be going, "Freedom! Americans!" And that's why we didn't need armor on the tanks because they'd be giving us flowers and chocolates and nylons.

Maher: New Rule: Stop whining about the French. It takes a lot of guts to stand up to the Bush administration, and that's more than I can say about the Democrats!

Maher: Seriously, Mr. President, this job can't be fun for you anymore. There's no more money to spend; you used up all of that. You can't start another war because you also used up the army.

Maher: New Rule: Traitors don't get to question my patriotism. What could be less patriotic than constantly screwing things up for America? You know, it's literally hard to keep up with the sheer volume of scandals in the Bush administration. Which is why I like to download the latest scandals right onto my iPod. That way, I can catch up on this week's giant fuckup on my drive into work. In fact, Bush has so many scandals, he could open a chain of Bush Scandal & Fuckup themed restaurants. Hmmm, should I get the Harriet Miers, the Meatloaf, or the Katrina Crabcakes? You know, not to generalize, but the 29 percent of people who still support President Bush are the ones who love to pronounce themselves more patriotic than the rest of us. But just saying you're patriotic is like saying you have a big cock. If you have to say it, chances are it's not true. And indeed, the party that flatters itself that they protect America better is the party that has exhausted the military, left the ports wide open, and purposely outed a CIA agent, Valerie Plame. That's not treason anymore? Outing a spy? Did I mention it was one of *our* spies? Mark Twain said, "Patriotism is supporting your country all the time, and your government when it deserves it." And I say Valerie Plame is a patriot because she spent her life serving her country. Scooter Libby is not, because he spent his life serving Dick Cheney. Valerie Plame kept her secrets. The Bush administration leaked like the plumbing at Walter Reed.[8]

Maher on Donald Trump

Regarding former US president Donald Trump, Maher laid out a scary undemocratic scenario in the hopes of arousing viewers from slumber. "I've been saying it ever since he lost," Maher warned. "He's like a shark that's not gone, just gone out to sea. But actually, he's been quietly eating people this whole time." Using a reference from *Game of Thrones*, a popular fantasy TV show in which power-hungry characters kill each other for the coveted Iron Throne, Maher clarifies his warning by saying, "And by eating people, I mean he has been methodically purging the Republican Party of anyone who voted for his impeachment or doesn't believe that he is the rightful leader of the Seven Kingdoms."[9]

Maher's (Imaginary) Eulogy to Trump

Dear family and frenemies of Donald Trump, some men look at the world and ask why. Donald Trump looked at the world and asked, "What's in it for me?" His generosity knew only limits, and he never failed to put himself before others. He was a devoted father who every day tried to teach his children the wrong lessons of life. . . . He once said that the experience of not being in Vietnam taught him the most important lesson of all: there's no problem so big you can't lie your way out of it. . . . Donald Trump never met a man he liked. . . . But as

192

a walking parody of himself, he was a challenge to satirize and made me a better comedian for it. He died as he lived: wearing makeup and lying in front of all of us, So fly free, whiny little bitch. Fly free. . . .[10]

It seems that when a system is not making appropriate responses to the feedback mechanisms that were created to maintain the balance necessary for self-preservation, the system develops new functions for altering itself so it can move forward. It develops new mechanisms for providing the data necessary for self-preservation.

Throughout the history of civilization, as the poor or evil behavior of those in power has been exposed, new sources of information have developed. Whether it be Thomas Paine during the American Revolution or the abolitionists before and during the Civil War, new voices have emerged to challenge their time. And when all else seems lost, jesters like Bill Maher come to our aid.

Conclusion

Evolutionary psychologists have said that the dominant biological force driving evolution is the passing of genes. Though this idea seems useful and is highly speculative, we have accepted the notion that biological species are driven to maintain themselves. Based on my observations, the two instinctive drives that support this contention are curiosity and love. After all, maintaining our kinship group allows us to preserve our genes. Obviously, love of our partner and love of our offspring are the two psychological requirements for continuing the species. Beyond love, there is a need to master our environment to bring safety to the clan. Mastery requires an instinctive need for curiosity. Without a push toward learning about the world and ourselves, our experience would quickly become stagnant and we would perish. The more our thoughts become rigid and ossified, the more we interfere with our natural inclinations.

The ideas expressed in this book are not particularly new or unique. Sigmund Freud understood how basic libido was necessary to the survival of our species. He ultimately chose it as the life force driving human survival, developing the idea of the "reality principle" to provide a mechanism for an individual's survival. His creation of defense mechanisms and, ultimately, the idea of ego mechanisms are metaphors for explaining a human's push toward preservation in a complex environment, The historical problem for Freud was that he was a physician and was forced to develop themes that were acceptable to the medical world. Unfortunately, this led to overly complex metaphors that were often incorrect. In fact, Freud himself understood that the human personality was better explored by professions other than medicine:

You often estimate me too highly. For I am not really a man of science, not an observer, not an experimenter, and not a thinker. I am nothing but a temperament a conquistador—an adventurer, if you want to translate the word—with the curiosity, the boldness and the tenacity that belong to that type of being. Such people are apt to be treasured if they succeed, if they really discovered something: otherwise, they are thrown aside. And that is not altogether unjust.[1]

Freud, the mentor of modem psychiatry, understood the limitations of his field. He also understood the value of love and curiosity. It was curiosity that drove him to his musings. Likewise, Robert Jay Lifton, in his book *The Protean Self*, grasped that if humans were going to succeed in the contemporary world, they needed to be flexible and adaptable.[2] In other words, for us to survive, we need to continue exploring and learning. We are all being continuously bombarded by proliferating information. Thus, we must have the capacity to learn and evolve in various situations.

However, Lifton also recognized the basic social nature of the human experience: "The overall quest involves a struggle for human connectedness, for ways of symbolizing immortality in the form of attachments that transcend one's limited life span."[3] From the inception of time, humans have been highly social animals. They joined together first in families, then in communities to provide experiences that will serve their shared needs for emotional bonds as well as safety and development.

The power of love in particular is undeniable. In his book *Love and Will*, Rollo May makes the case that love is the most powerful mechanism for affirming our existence. Anyone who has ever experienced this emotion recognizes its power. Additionally, love is not simply an internal personal state. As May suggests, just being in the other person's presence moves us into a space that is memorable and extraordinary. Our body tingles, our internal temperature rises, our face flushes, and our heart pounds. We may also witness similar phenomena taking place in our lover. This is a mutually constructed social experience. It can and does not exist in a vacuum. The notion of being in love requires a loved object.[4]

Though we can love from afar—and though love can be unrequited—at its most potent, this experience is mutual and reciprocal. The experience and intensity of love are magnified through the reflexive process of continued dialogue and sharing.

Love can take many forms. The experience of adult romantic love is inordinately powerful, but so is the experience of a mother's love for her child. Even before birth, a mother is developing bonds with her unborn child. As pointed out by psychologists such as E.H. Erikson and John Bowlby, a child learns the power of attachment through their early relationship with their mother. Erikson in particular noted that the adult stage of development is the age of generativity. According to his writings, a parent derives satisfaction from their posture of being nurturing and giving. It is the child's responsibility to be the passive recipient of this succoring. Thus, the mother derives satisfaction through her loving and giving.[5]

Throughout this book, we have discovered that the archetypes of love run deeply in Western culture. However, from the inception of our culture's discussion of love and collaboration, power and control have seeped into and superseded that discussion. As noted during chapter one, in the original story of creation, Lilith seeks out God to gain the power position over Adam in lovemaking. God responds that Adam (or "Man") will be the more powerful. But what if God had said to Lilith, "I understand your frustration, but it is your and Adam's responsibility to work out these problems"? What if he had told her, "It is your responsibility to love each other"? What if our ancestors were less concerned with power and more concerned with love? After all, weren't these myths and fables created to control us? Freud had said that it is our drive toward aggression that has caused society to create its cultural mandates. Though this may be partly true, it seems that our fear of love may be equally at the source of many of our cultural prohibitions. It may even be that the frustration of our needs with love is our source of aggression.

Though wise folks and leaders of the Judeo-Christian tradition have always understood the importance of love, their messages have often gone unheeded. Approximately two or three decades before Jesus, Rabbi Hillel taught his wisdom at the Beit Hillel, a school for teachers. These are probably his two best-known statements:

If I am not for myself, then who will be for me? And when I am only for myself, what am I? And if not now, when? (Pirkei Avot I:14)

That which is hateful to you, do not do to your neighbor. (That is the whole Torah; the rest is the explanation. I recommend that you read the Babylonian Talmud, Tractate Shabbat 31a. See in particular the ethic of reciprocity, or the "Golden Rule.")

Several decades later, the Jews were fighting among themselves for control of religious practice. It was Jesus who reminded them of Rabbi Hillel's concerns. Love, after all, was Jesus's first and foremost concern. When he was being questioned by the Pharisees, one of them tested him by asking, "Teacher, which commandment in the law is the greatest?" Jesus answered by reciting from the holiest of ancient Hebrew chants:

You shall love the Lord, your God with all your heart, with all your soul and with all your mind. This is the greatest and the first commandment. The second is like it: You shall love your neighbor as yourself. The whole law and the prophets depend on these two commandments. (Mathew 22:34-39, with parallelism from Mark and Luke)

Unfortunately, within 300 to 400 years of Jesus's death, the codification of the religion of his followers was tainted by the Roman emperor Constantine's need for order in the empire. The discussion of ideas—in particular, love—was subservient to the need for power and control. According to James Carroll in his book *Constantine's Sword*, Christian theology—much like that of Judaism—was characterized by discussion and multiplicity of meaning. However, after Constantine, multiplicity of meaning became heresy. The ideas that became the basis of the Catholic Church were rooted in politics, not theology. Thus, Constantine became the leader of the political realm as well as the spiritual realm.[6]

The word *heresy* comes from the Greek word *hairesis*, or *choose*. In the case of Christian theology, it implies the choice of those who believe or those who are dissident. Ironically, Jesus himself was a dissident. Yet those who codified the Christian theology seemingly couldn't tolerate others who behaved in Jesus's questioning manner.

Earlier, in chapters four and six, we discussed Irenaeus of Lyon. His lack of confidence in early Christians seems to be at the root of the codification of Christianity. Until recently, his demagoguery,

Against Heresies, was the only testimony to the early Gnostic beliefs. Irenaeus was determined to keep Gnostic ideas out of the emerging Christian theology. Furthermore, he was the individual who proffered the idea that the canonical Gospels were divinely inspired.

Irenaeus sent Christianity on the tact of obedience rather than love. Power and control were to supplant the paramount message of Jesus, to "love God with all your heart." Irenaeus saw Jesus as he knew Adam, who systematically undid what Adam had done. He believed that Jesus was the obedient son of God who came to save humanity from original sin. He also preached that Mary, unlike her predecessor Eve, had faith; she didn't "question" God's word. Additionally, Irenaeus didn't accept those who challenged the idea of the unity of God. His theology was steeped in faith and obedience. Through his efforts and other Church hierarchy, the ideas of the early Gnostic writers were lost to society for most of the next 2,000 years. Important concepts suggesting a theology based on collaboration and dialogue disappeared. This included the idea that the Jesus of the Gnostic tradition knows God by looking inward as well as through teachings, and that he believes in his ideas and is willing to discuss with others the merit of these ideas.

Ironically, despite the efforts of cultural forces to subdue the power of love, that power is celebrated every week in churches and synagogues. People's prayers are often for peace and justice in the world. They ask God for forgiveness of their trespasses against others and celebrate the oneness of God and his peoples. This is seen in the following prayer from the Unitarian Prayer Book:

A prayer for Tolerance! May we remember in our Humanity

We are part of a world family.

Tolerance Noting differences

While remaining peaceful. Recognizing that each has the right

To determine their reality.

Tolerance Allowing us to remain calm

When we think others should act differently.

Tolerance breeding happiness As we take tender insights Into living. Tolerance blossoming in peace, joy, happiness, love Acceptance in love by practicing love.

Amen

At times of prayer, especially prayers such as the one shared above, parishioners experience deep feelings of spirituality. People often express the feeling of the moment as a longing for connection to both a higher power and their community. Where, then, is the deep longing for love rooted? If Freud was correct, culture was needed to promote the ideas promulgated in such prayer. Yet, in my experience, the spiritual moments reached in the houses of worship around the world are reflections of a deeply internal, genetically programmed need for kinship and community. In other words, it is the natural drive of humankind to love and be loved.

Over the past two millennia, very few leaders have stood up for the power of love. Time and time again, those who have attempted to bring society back to values and principles rooted in compassion and community have been vilified or destroyed by the forces of power and control. Beginning with Jesus's crucifixion, those who have stood up for love and justice have found themselves in danger. Examples of other great leaders who have railed against the tyranny of power are Martin Luther King Jr. and Mahatma Gandhi. They mobilized great movements in their times, only to be assassinated.

Each of these great leaders understood that, at least in part, the answer to seeking the salvation of humanity—and, for that matter, the world—was by establishing a culture that was imbued with love and always questioned authority. Now, it is not my contention that we can live in a world that has no rules or authority. Rather, authority is a categorical imperative, an ultimate truth. However, the authorities are often wrong. Throughout this book, we have witnessed people in power, at all levels of social organization, struggling to maintain that power. As Lord Acton, the British historian, noted over a century ago, "Power tends to corrupt and absolute power corrupts absolutely."[7]

From our culture's beginnings, we have seen those in control developing social rules and mores that perpetuate the status quo. In the Gospel of Thomas, for instance, Jesus tells us that he was the serpent. He had come to Earth to warn us that the Hebrew god had a special interest in humankind but that this god didn't want us to experience the truth about the Universe. This god was one of the many angels of the seraphim. Even in the apocryphal tale of Lilith, where our ancestors were more willing to discuss the nature of sociosexual politics, the allegory continues the perpetuation of male empowerment.

We have also seen the effort to distort our thinking reflected in corporate language and organization. This language and thinking are regularly seen in the corridors of our government. We have even seen it play out in the politics of psychotherapy. The medical model continues because it is in the best interest of doctors and other ancillary medical professionals to continue fostering it. Research from the 1960s onward, however, has questioned the efficacy of this paradigm.

The seeds of evil are being sown about us. Unsurprisingly, in countries like Bolivia and Venezuela, people are looking to populist leaders such Evo Morales, Nicolas Maduro, and Hugo Chávez to lead them against the oppressive power structure. Like in many other countries throughout the world, these populations have suffered from neglect and abuse. However, the binary structure of our culture has left them outside the benefits of the world's economic resources. And, unfortunately, multinational corporations are quickly mobilizing their allies to disarm their opponents. In these instances, we are already hearing the language that evilizes those who repudiate the people in charge.

Governments, corporate structures, and even professional organizations attempt to control information in their own best interest. Regulating agencies are complicit with corporate entities such as Verizon to keep important information out of the hands of employees and stockholders. The newspapers are full of blatant examples of corporate malfeasance. We have all watched as the Kenneth Lays of the world have been caught in their efforts to preserve their wealth. Corporate leaders take care of their own needs while diminishing the interests of those who depend on them to maintain their fiduciary responsibility.

However, we often overlook those who are responsible for our physical or mental health in their self-serving efforts to maintain power. How often is pecuniary logic the basis for decision-making in medicine? How often is new medical technology brought to the general public and then owned by those who are meant to make it so accessible? Frequently, the cost of health could be reduced by providing models of delivery based on the needs of the community rather than that of the providers. Think of why communities might raise money to buy or develop ice rinks but not electronic imaging equipment, or why Americans allow their federal government to prohibit less expensive Canadian medicines from being imported into the country. Apparently, those who are aware of the problems and their solutions often keep us from having full knowledge of the situation.

Similarly, the paradigms governing the assessment and treatment of individuals with emotional problems have been dominated by the medical model. Those who are aware of the research conducted during the community mental health movement of the 1960s and '70s know that a therapist's personality variables are far more important in outcome studies than their theoretical position.[8, 9, 10] How many people realize that Erik Erikson, the well-known psychoanalyst, was an artist with no formal education in psychotherapy? Why did Anna Freud (daughter of Sigmund Freud) continue supporting the cult of psychoanalysis when she knew fully that medical education was superfluous to the process? Why is a psychotherapist's taxonomy so dominated by obtuse language that it makes ideas inaccessible? It seems that in all fields and endeavors, information is withheld to maintain the status quo of those in power.

Our questions and concerns will go on and on. Suffice it to say, we have lost our way in the evolutionary development of our culture.

The original genetic predisposition toward love and curiosity has been supplanted by the forces of power and control. The original human impetus toward a community based on caring and learning seems to have been replaced by the imperative of individual well-being. Society has become egocentric in its focus. The value of taking care of our world and our community has been replaced by a cult of conspicuous consumption.

We are now at a critical point of human evolution. Our world's resources are being taxed to the breaking point. Unless we reevaluate our cultural mandates—and unless we return to our original genetic directions—the world will fall victim to evildoing. Our destiny requires that we reassert our internally prescribed drives of love and curiosity.

Postscript: Spinning

Anyone who is familiar with postmodernism realizes that there is never a conclusion. We must move on beyond what appears to be the book's last chapter. Thinking, of course, is evolutionary; it continues to develop, change, and unfold. By living in a world of instant communication dominated by television, we have to reflect on at least one more aspect of the general construction of ideas.

Today's contentious environment requires the belief in one more chapter. Contemporary culture is faced with the extraordinary problem of having too much expert commentary and too few experts. As the nightly news is being delivered to us, so-called experts appear on TV to tell us what to think and how to understand the events we have just witnessed. The same dozen or so pundits appear on several channels, shaping the construction of our thoughts.

Postmodernists, as noted often in this book, believe that truth is dialogic and socially constructed by the participants of the dialogue. Thus, the power of television—and, to a lesser extent, radio and print media—is massive.

This is not a new idea. However, what is increasingly apparent is that a decreasing number of these so-called experts are participating in the discussion. Furthermore, the time between event and commentary has become instantaneous. How can the masses be expected to understand a presidential address or come to an opinion on the Middle East without David Gergen, George Mitchell, Sean Hannity, or Ann Coulter telling us what to think?

Many television analysts are bright and entertaining. However, we are left with little time to sit back and reflect on the events around us. When I was younger, my family would often share a discussion after reading the morning paper. Even the horrors of the Vietnam War entered our personnel space hours or days after the events took place. Today, embedded journalists are broadcasting to us from the front lines as the war occurs. We have watched Katyusha rockets shot off by Hezbollah troops strike in Israel moments later. Would we even believe that these events were happening if it weren't for the likes of Anderson Cooper or Tucker Carlson? If they weren't on hand to annotate the events, could we possibly comprehend what is happening before our eyes? Do all of today's events require the presence of a play-by-play commentator? Cooper, for example, was on hand to show us the horrors of Hurricane Katrina. Another time, he was embedded in Iraq, Israel, and Heathrow Airport within the same week. What happened to all the other correspondents? Why are we continuously narrowing down the sources of our information? What has become of our capability to make independent judgments about world events?

The concept of witness and dialogue are central to the practice of postmodern psychotherapy. In my psychotherapy practice, my colleagues and I often have witness or reflecting teams participating in the treatment. These teams carefully listen to the dialogues taking place during the psychotherapy sessions, then thicken and broaden the discussion. They listen to family members sharing their concerns. After about fifteen or twenty minutes, the reflecting team discusses issues, stories, and themes that emerged during the discussion. As a therapist, it often surprises me to hear the ideas I didn't notice during the previous discussion. At times, these reflecting teams even include family members. In fact, we often include the identified child patient on these teams.

In one clinical example, a fourteen-year-old boy was referred to my practice after he was excluded from an inpatient psychiatric unit. We were told by the hospital that he was too disruptive to the psychiatric unit to continue his stay. Can you imagine a fourteen-year-old child who is too oppositional to be treated? He bore the labels my colleagues and I now regularly see in children who are referred to us: oppositional defiant disorder, attention deficit disorder, and possibly bipolar disorder. Additionally, the boy had previously been excluded from school for being too disruptive and dangerous.

During the first treatment session, my team and I asked the boy to assist us with the treatment of his family and to be part of the treatment team. He immediately asked, "Are you asking me to be a doctor?"

"Actually, yes," I responded.

Surprisingly, the boy sat and listened to his parents discuss their family history for about half an hour. He listened intently without being challenging or disruptive. He listened to his mother as she spoke of the pain she had experienced since the death of her mother. He listened to her feelings of being let down by her husband. He listened to his father's frustration of always falling short in his wife's eyes. He listened to how his father, as well as his mother, realized how much their relationship had changed since the grandmother's death.

Following his parents' dialogue, the boy immediately spoke up: "Excuse me. Do you mind if I speak first? I really have an important thought. Is it possible that I became disruptive because my mother was depressed? Did anyone else notice that my problems started when my grandmother died and my mother started taking antidepressants? Is that possible? I never noticed that before."

One of my colleagues on the treatment team said, "That's an interesting idea! Why do you think that you might not have noticed that before?"

"Well, other than me being so disruptive?"

"Yeah."

"I don't think anyone has put everything together. It's always been my problem." The boy kept shaking his head as if in disbelief. "Wow. Do you think it's possible that I'm not crazy?"

Shortly afterward, I asked the parents to reflect on their son's thoughts. His mother immediately began to cry. "He hasn't participated like that in a long time," she said. "I really had begun to think that he was crazy. He's like the kid I remember."

"We haven't talked to each other for a long while," the boy's dad reflected. "I agree with my son: we haven't had time or distance to put it all together."

The therapy session allowed the family to engage with one another. Its structure facilitated listening and collaboration between parents and child. All three family members, with the help of the reflecting dialogue, put ideas together in previously unconsidered ways. New possibilities for understanding their dynamics quickly emerged.

The idea of reflection and commentary on the news is an old, once-useful tradition. If the spirit of dialogue was to discuss and open us to new ways of thinking, it could be useful again. It might even be useful to listen to people question each other in the pursuit of new and interesting ways of solving problems. However, today's media seems to pander to either the public or powerful interest groups. The major difference between the reflecting dialogues of a therapy session and an expert's discussion on television is that the therapy dialogues are meant to open the group to new possibilities and thinking. The discussions and debates in the media, however, heighten and polarize differences at best and attempt to shape our thinking at worst.

Spinning has actually become a profession. Political consultants are hired by candidates for office to package and present their ideas and political platforms. Unfortunately, those who are responsible for presenting these opposing positions also change the facts regarding their opponents' lives and ideas. Karl Rove, who was often thought of as George W. Bush's brain, takes the liberty of presenting any "truth" he thinks will sell in Peoria. More recently, Kellyanne Conway has turned Rove's tactic into an art form. Today's political consultants have no problem making ad hominem attacks on opponents. Is it wrong—even bordering on evil—for the opposing campaign to show a foolish picture of Michael Dukakis in a tank? When does spinning achieve the level of evil? Is it evil to challenge John Kerry's record as a Vietnam veteran? Or to sell the idea of weapons of mass destruction when the overwhelming evidence suggests they don't exist?

In this complex world we live in, it is important to be open to the possibility of alternative perspectives. Unfortunately, with the rise of fundamentalist thinking, the opposite trend seems to be in vogue. The general assumption being promulgated in our culture is that our beliefs are paramount and true. The converse is also assumed; those who oppose our ideals are wrong. Interestingly, we all seem to recognize the fallacy of this position when mutual opponents such as Osama bin Laden state it. And when postmodern therapists take on the stance of alternative perspectives, it leads to reduced tension in families and can be useful in creating new dialogues between communities and peoples.

The problem is much more pervasive than the narrowing down of experts in the media, though. It is apparent that, from one US presidential administration to the next, the same people are retreaded to function in new policy positions. In a country of over 300 million people, only several dozen are deemed qualified to lead us. Whether those individuals are Democrats or Republicans, we watch the same cast of characters reemerge to solve the world's problems. The same old beliefs and philosophies are continuously recycled to contend with emerging issues and concerns. How many times will Dick Cheney or William Barr be called back to government service? We have even witnessed the reemergence of Henry Kissinger. How many times will society suffer through solutions that lack creativity or ingenuity?

We can't seem to find new wine—or even new bottling for the old wine. Is it possible that the hallowed halls of Harvard, Yale, or Stanford have taken the best and brightest and turned them into "task idiots"? Are the graduates of these highly thought-of universities serving the gods of modernism and not learning new ways to think and act in our quickly evolving world? Ironically, the basis for criticizing the Trump administration was substantiated by the fact that experts on the World Affairs Councils of America found that the administration's foreign policy and strategies were lacking. Those policies and strategies were also being carried out by individuals— mostly men—who had previously served in positions such as US Secretary of State or at high levels of the CIA or the State Department and had failed at developing cogent world policy. What is it about our culture that has us continuously dipping into the same tainted wells?

The dialogues within government need new breath. There is a need for expanded thinking and the development of new possibilities. The process of government seems to reify an administration's policy even when it is clearly wrong. What keeps a man like Colin Powell from coming forward and challenging the failed policy of the administration he worked for? What is it about our system that causes governments to spin tales about failed policy rather than be forthright and change direction?

Similarly, as hurricane after hurricane has struck the US Gulf Coast, we have watched live television demonstrate the government's failure to care for the people of that region. And as we witnessed one catastrophe after another unfold, President Donald Trump used a

Sharpie to alter a hurricane's track so it was more compatible with his narrative. Do the requirements of modernism preclude ever being wrong? Do we expect those in government—or even ourselves—to always be correct?

What we do expect, however, is for the President of the United States to tell us the truth. We expect that our country's government will provide us with clear information about the issues affecting our lives. And we ultimately expect those in government to be beneficent and seek proper solutions to the many problems that regularly confront us.

Though postmodernism assumes that knowledge is socially constructed, it also assumes that there are consensually validated and useful truths. Additionally, it recognizes that there are many valid and interesting stances to confronting problems. Our concern is that, while exploring the issues of life, we are presented with the information necessary to come to valid conclusions. It is assumed that people can have frank, open discussions and still affirm one another.

One of the lessons of postmodern therapy is that people can work together to find new solutions. Being open to other perspectives and views can lead to many new possibilities and a shared understanding. Postmodernism recognizes that truth is illusive and evolutionary in nature. Though previous history and cultural bias can confound truth, the process of inquiry and collaboration leaves open the hope for the development of successful solutions to problems.

Postmodern therapy can be a model for constructive social change. In a world of ever-shifting dynamics, there is still a need for a process that is respectful of opposing views and realities. Unfortunately, modernism has become too stagnant and offers conclusions that are too limiting. Modernism has us praying to false gods. The time is right for the continued development of a process that is steeped in curiosity, is open to new possibilities, seeks to reinvigorate old ideas, and operates within a framework of love and affirmation. The time is right for understanding the possibility that God is yet to be born.

Denouement: The Axis of Evil

This is not truly a denouement. Unfortunately, there will never be a denouement to this discussion. Each time we believe there is a possible conclusion to this narrative, another Putin or Trump emerges. It seemed as though every time I appeared to have finished this book, more examples of evil in our world became evident.

As I write this, it is February 2022, and the world is witnessing the horror of evil in Ukraine. Russian troops and tanks have entered a sovereign country that has done the Russians no harm. Under false pretenses and claims, innocent people are being subjected to bombs and mayhem. We are watching as Russia—or, rather, Vladimir Putin—perpetrates .wanton destruction upon civilian populations. Once again, all the conditions for evildoing are evident. How painful it is to note that, throughout the history of civilization, the conditions for evildoing persist?

The speech given by Putin on February 21, 2022 is full of misinformation and false narratives. It offers a pretext, however, for engaging in power over behavior against the Ukrainian people. Ironically, on one hand, Putin attempted to legitimize his actions by arguing that he was saving the Ukrainians from past historical errors made by the Bolsheviks, who separated the Russian people living in the provinces labeled as Ukraine from their true heritage in Russia.

He then attempted to portray Ukrainians as the other, calling them neo-Nazis. Of course, no one can kill their own people without labeling them as the other.

It is also important to note that Putin's justifications for his actions included how the West had caused evil in the past. He made this claim during his speech on February 21, which has been translated to English:

But the example that stands apart from the above events is, of course, the invasion of Iraq without any legal grounds. They used the pretext of allegedly reliable information available in the United States about the presence of weapons of mass destruction in Iraq. To prove that allegation, the US Secretary of State held up a vial with white power, publicly, for the whole world to see, assuring the international community that it was a chemical warfare agent created in Iraq. It later turned out that all of that was a fake and a sham, and that Iraq did not have any chemical weapons. Incredible and shocking but true. We witnessed lies made at the highest state level and voiced from the high UN rostrum. As a result, we see a tremendous loss in human life, damage, destruction, and a colossal upsurge of terrorism.[1]

It is inconceivable that one would label the actions of another as evil, then use it as justification for their own poor behavior. Of course, all of the earmarks of evil exist in Putin's speech. As shown in the above quote as well as the following excerpts, he presented misinformation over and over again while justifying his actions. He also distorted reality to his end and offered the most simplistic and dangerous solutions to reach his end goal:

They will undoubtedly try to bring war to Crimea, just as they have done in Donbass: to kill innocent people, just as members of the punitive units of Ukrainian nationalists and Hitler's accomplices did during the Great Patriotic War. They have also openly laid claim to several other Russian regions.

If we look at the sequence of events and the incoming reports, the showdown between Russia and these forces cannot be avoided. It is only a matter of time. They are getting ready and waiting for the right moment. Moreover, they went as far as aspire to acquire nuclear weapons. We will not let this happen. . . .

The purpose of this operation is to protect people who, for eight years now, have been facing humiliation and genocide perpetrated by the Kiev regime. To this end, we will seek to demilitarize and denazify Ukraine, as well as bring to trial those who perpetrated numerous bloody crimes against civilians, including against citizens of the Russian Federation. . . .[2]

It is not sensible to portray Ukraine as a Nazi threat or a danger to Russia. After all, it was Russia who invaded Crimea in 2014. Russian proxies have also militarized the eastern provinces of Ukraine. Above all, the Ukrainian people—along with the Russians—were killed by the millions by the Nazis. It is also important to note that the free people of Ukraine elected a Jewish man, Volodymyr Zelenskyy, as their president.

Unimaginably, a large portion of the US Republican Party is following the lead of Donald Trump and Fox News by blaming President Biden, rather than criticizing Putin. Tucker Carlson called upon Americans to turn their backs on our government's position and support Putin. He even praised Putin while disparaging American heroes such as Alexander Vindman. Vindman, of course, was the lieutenant colonel who exposed Trump's phone call about Ukraine. As usual, the facts about Trump's behavior have been distorted. He has been portrayed as a tough leader who stood up to Putin. "This could never have happened while Trump was President."[3] There is no acknowledgment, however, that Trump continuously appeased Putin.

In 2018, Trump reportedly spent two hours in a room alone with Putin, save for a pair of interpreters. He then said this during a joint news conference with Putin: "I have great confidence in my intelligence people, but I will tell you that President Putin was extremely strong and powerful in his denial today."[4]

One must remember that Trump was impeached for his attempts to extort the Ukrainian president. This wouldn't have happened under Trump, because Putin would have been appeased by him. Thus, an axis of evil exists between Trump and Putin. This is further evidenced in the following statement from Trump during an interview on *The Clay Travis and Buck Sexton Show*: "I went in yesterday, and there was a television screen, and I said, 'This is genius.' Putin declares a big portion of the Ukraine . . . Putin declares it as independent. . . ." He continued praising Putin's invasion, saying that "This is genius" and "How smart is that?" He also mentioned that this was how Americans should behave on the US-Mexico border.[5]

Clearly, both Trump and Putin are interested in being powerful autocrats. The idea of free dialogue and shared leadership is anathema to them. Oddly enough, the first US president, George Washington, had magnanimously refused to be a king. Now, over 200 years later, a recently former US president has attempted to overturn the country's national elections and install himself as monarch. Trump, much like Putin, is interested in promoting nationalistic movements that mimic Hitler's Nazi slogans "Blood and soil!" and "You will not replace us!"

Putin has been on a long campaign to disrupt the Western allies and diminish the power of democratic dialogue. His goal has been to restore the Russian empire—the Soviet Union—to prominence. His strategy for this has included all four mechanisms that lead to evil. He appears to be obsessed with keeping the world divided and shows no interest in joining the Western economic or value system. He has also attempted to distort and misrepresent facts with fictions by regularly using the Internet to pose "alternative facts." He is much more terrified of ideas than he is of NATO. Now, in his invasion of Ukraine, Putin has clearly demonstrated a simplistic solution to the complex problem of dealing with human aspiration. War—a form of power over behavior—has always mobilized those who people in power oppose to resist.

Wittingly or unwittingly, Trump has joined with Putin in his efforts to subvert and divide our country. He has been the recipient of Putin's efforts to undo both the 2016 and 2020 US national elections. He has even joined with Putin in promoting narratives that keep the populace at odds with one another. For instance, Trump and his spokespeople frequently promote alternative facts. His supporters are continuously encouraged to delegitimize our electoral system. Trump has been an outspoken supporter of Putin; and together, these two men have formed an axis of evil, intent on disrupting democracy and advancing authoritarianism.

Freedom is precarious. It requires that the general public remain diligent to the signs of danger. Thus, we must always be alert to evildoing. Once again, we must be aware of the indicators of behavior that lead to the construction of evil. We are at the precipice; and unless we can demonstrate to Trump and his supporters that we understand their anger and wish to unite in finding solutions to the concerns and dangers around us, we will degenerate into chaos and war.

Notes and Bibliography

Chapter One: The Problem

2.   Graves et al, Hebrew Myths.The Book of Genesis Chapter 9 Doubleday NY 1964

Barbara G. Walker, *The Woman's Encyclopedia of Myths and Secrets* (New York: HarperCollins, 1986p541

Sigmund Freud, *Civilization and its Discontents*, trans. James Strachey (New York: W. W. Norton & Company, 1989),

Albert Einstein quote on page 16.

Beyer, Landon and Liston, *Educational Theory Volume 42*, Fall *1992 University of Illinois p371393.*

Chapter Two: How Do We Define Evil?

3.   Elliot Aronson, *The Social Animal* (New York: W. H. Freeman and Company, 1988), p87

Saul Levine, "The Development of Wickedness—From Whence does Evil Stem?", *Psychiatric Annals* 27, no. 9 (1997): [insert page number(s)], p187 https://doi.org/10.3928/0048-5713-19970901-08.

Morris, 1997.Wickedness Mental Disorder and the LawPsychiatric annals Sept 1997 p638-660

Quote from *Frontline* episode in 2005.

Forensic Psychiatry and Medicine, 2005.

Forensic Psychiatry and Medicine, 2005.

Citation for the source of "the general vices of infidelity, ambition and lust."Kramer, heinrch , Sprenger,Jacob. Malleaus Mallicoforum in translation by Maxwell Sturt, Manchester UNiv Press2007 p.30

.Graves Warning to Children in Complete Book of Poems Penquin Books NY 2003 p.230Gr

Chapter Three: Binary Thinking

4.   Aristotle quote about slaves as "living tools."4Polotics I 4 1254, 1-13

5.   Joseph Campbell, *Occidental Mythology: The Masks of God*, revised edition (New York: Penguin Books, 1991), [insert page number(s)].

6.   Christopher B. Daly, "Salvi Convicted of Murder in Shootings," *The Washington Post*, March 19, 1996, A01.

7.   First quote from Berkowitz's letter to Captain Borrelli, 1977.

8.	Ibid.

9.	Michel Foucault, *Madness and Civilization: A History of Insanity in the Age of Reason*, (New York: Vintage Books, 1961pxiv

10.	Ibidpxv

11.	Maria Ressa quote from February 26, 2004.

12.	Andrew S. Clyde quotes from pages 37 and 38.

13.	Alexandria Ocasio-Cortez quote from page 38.

Chapter Four: The Limiting of Information

14.	Sophocles quote from page 40.

Galileo quote from 1633, found on page 41.

Elaine Pagels, *The Gnostic Gospels* (New York: Random House, 1979),

Ibid

15.	Saint Augustine, *The Literal Meaning of Genesis*, trans. John H. Taylor, Ancient Christian Writers, Vol. 41 and 42 (Insert Publication City: Newman Press, 1982), [insert page number(s)].

Quote from Jesus in the Gnostic Gospel of Thomas, found on page 45.

16.   Harlene Anderson and Harold A. Goolishian, "Human Systems as Linguistic Systems: Preliminary and Evolving Ideas about the Implications for Clinical Theory," *Family Process* 27, no. 4 (1988Kenneth J. Gergen and John Kaye, "Beyond Narrative in the Negotiation of Meaning," in *Therapy as Social Construction*, ed. Kenneth J. Gergen and Sheila McName*e (London, Uni*ted Kingdom: Sage Publications, 1992), p167

Ibid, [insert page number(s)]pP171

Tom Andersen, "The Reflecting Team: Dialogue and Meta-Dialogue in Clinical Work," *Family Process* 26, no. 4 (December 1987): [insert page number(s)*], pp33*https://doi.org/10.1111/j.1545-5300.1987.00415.x.

Saint Augustine, *Confessions*, trans. Henry Chadwick (New York: Oxford University Press, 1991), .p 2

Ludwig Wittgenstein, *Tractatus Logico Philosophicus*, trans. D. F. Pears and B. F. McGuinness (Insert Publication City: Humanities Press, 1974), 122.

Quote from Sean Illing *Vox* article dated 03/22/2019.

Quote from Thomas B. Edsall article from unknown source, 12/15/2016.

Scottie Nell Hughes quote from *The Diane Rehm Show,* November 30,

Sidney Powell quotes from pages 50 and 51.

Chapter Five: Simple Solutions to Complex Problems

17.   James Hansen quotes and information, page 53.

Chapter Six: Power Over Behavior

18.   Freud, *Civilization and Its Discontentsp 65*

Caligula quote from page 63.

Foucault, *Madness and Civilization: A History of Insanity in the Age of Reason*, [insert page number(s)].

Foucault quote from 1980, found on page 64.

Leo Strauss, *The City and Man* (Chicago, Illinois: University of Chicago Press, 1978), 5.

Ibid, p 6

Trump quote from 2018 article in *The New York Times*.

Quote from Glen Kessler article in *The Washington Post,* November 2018.

Corey Lewandowski quote from page 71.

Gretchen Morgenson, "[Insert Title of Article]," *The New York Times*, April 10, 2006,

Ibid.

Verizon, internal memo to employees, April 11, 2006.

Ibid.

Anderson and Goolishian, "Human Systems as Linguistic Systems: Preliminary and Evolving Ideas about the Implications for Clinical Theory," 467.

Chapter Seven: The Convergence

19.   Sir Thomas More quote from page 82.

20.   Hitler, 1922.

21.   Miloš Forman (director), *One Flew Over the Cuckoo's Nest,* 1975, Beverly Hills, CA: United Artists.

22.   Ibid.

23.   Ibid.

Chapter Eight: The Special Problem of Physiology

24.   Joseph Glenmullen, Prozac Backlash: *Overcoming the Dangers of Prozac, Zoloft, Paxil, and Other Antidepressants with Safe, Effective Alternatives* (New York: Simon & Schuster, 2000 Carey Goldberg, "Antidepressant appr*oval system criticized," The Boston   Globe,   April   23,   2004,* http://www.antidepressantsfacts.com/2004-04-23-Antidep-approval-sys-criticized.htm.

David Healey, "Lines of Evidence on the Risks of Suicide with Selective Serotonin Reuptake Inhibitors," *Psychotherapy and Psychosomatics* 72, no. 2 (2003): [insert page number(s)], https://doi.org/10.1159/000068691.

Vera H. Sharav, letter from the Alliance for Human Research Protection to Thomas R. Insel, MD, June 22, 2004.

Chapter Nine: Fundamentalism, or the Age of Dogma

25.   Governor John Winthrop quote from page 104.

26.   Emma Lazarus, "The New Colossus," 1883, as inscribed on the plaque of the Statue of Liberty.

27.   Wittgenstein quote from page 107.

28.   Gergen and Kaye, "Beyond Narrative in the Negotiation of Meaning," *Therapy as Social Construction*, p167.

29.	Burge, "[Insert Title of Article]," *The New York Times*, October 8, 2021

Chapter Ten: Sexual Perversity

30.	2015 *Psychology Today* article reporting statistics on Internet pornography, found on pages 110 and 111.

31.	Survivor Connections study information found on page 111.

32.	Wisconsin Coalition Against Sexual Assault report referenced on page 111.

33.	Rebbe Nachman, Union of Hebrew Congregations Workbook, 31.

34.	Michel Foucault, *The History of Sexuality* (Insert Publication City: Publisher, Year of Publication), [insert page number(s)].

35.	James Miller, unidentified source, page 115.

36.	Ruth Mazo Karras, "Active/Passive, Acts/Passions: Greek and Roman Sexualities," *The American Historical Review* 105, No. 4 (October 2000), https://www.jstor.org/stable/2651412.

37.	Saint Augustine-related quotes and paraphrased information from page 116.

38.   Saint Augustine, *On Marriage and Concupiscence* (Insert Publication City: Publisher, Year of Publication), [insert page number(s)].

39.   Michael Hammer's University of Arizona research, paraphrased content on page 117.

Chapter Eleven: What Is Thinking?

40.   Anderson and Goolishian, "Human Systems as Linguistic Systems: Preliminary and Evolving Ideas about the Implications for Clinical Theory," [insert page number(s)].

Jerome Bruner, among others, paraphrased and quoted content on page 122.

John Dougherty, "It Practices What They Preach," *The Phoenix New Times,* May 25, 2006, https://www.phoenixnewtimes.com/news/it-practices-what-they-preach-6401127.

Theodosius Dobzhansky, "A Geneticist's View of Human Equality," *Pharos Alpha Omega Alpha* 29 (1966): [insert page number(s)].

Robert Jay Lifton, *The Protean Self: Human Resilience in An Age of Fragmentation* (Chicago, Illinois: University of Chicago Press, 1999),

Ibid, [insert page number(s)].

Harry Stack Sullivan, *The Interpersonal Theory of Psychiatry* (New York: W. W. Norton & Company, 1953.,

Chapter Twelve: The Other

41.   Margoroh Maruyama paraphrased content on page 134.

42.   President George W. Bush quote on page 136.

43.   Émile Durkheim paraphrased content on page 137.

Chapter Thirteen: Puck the Jester, or Bill Maher

44.   Transcript of Bill Maher and Larry King on *Larry King Live* on page 146.

45.   William Shakespeare, *A Midsummer Night's Dream*, ed. [Insert names of editors, if there are any] (Insert Publication City: Publisher, Year of Publication), [insert act, scene, and line/stanza number(s)].

46.   Nat Binn, "Just for laughs, panel looks at what's funny, what's not," *The Newport Daily News*, June [insert date], 2003, [insert URL or print page number].

47.   Ibid.

48.   Lewis Black quote on pages 148 and 149.

49.   John Stewart quote from the Peabody Awards on page 152.

50.   Start separate citations for "Bill Maher on Religion" excerpts here .CNNLarry King 05/24/2002

51.   Start separate citations for "Maher on Bush and the Iraq War" excerpts here.on Real Time 09/29/2008

52.   Bill Maher quotes found in "Maher on Donald Trump."HBO rReal Timem,0807/2020

53.   Excerpt from Bill Maher's (imaginary) eulogy to Trump.In the Daily Kos 03/282007

Conclusion

54.   Ernest Jones, *The Life and Work of Sigmund Freud, Vol. 1.: The Formative Years and the Great Discoveries, 1856-1900* (London, United Kingdom: Hogarth Press, 1953), [insert page number(s)].

55.   Lifton, *The Protean Self*, [insert page number(s)].

56.   Ibid, page 6.

57.   Rollo May, *Love and Will* (Insert Publication City: Publisher, 1969

58.   Erik H. Erikson, *Childhood and Society* (New York: W. W. Norton & Company, 1968),

59.   James Carroll, *Constantine's Sword: The Church and the Jews, A History* (Boston, Massachusetts: Houghton Mifflin, 2001

60.   Lord Acton quote on page 165.

61.   Whitehorn and Betz paraphrased content on page 167.

62.   Rogers paraphrased content on page 167.

63.   Karkoff and Berenson paraphrased content on page 167.

Denouement: The Axis of Evil

64.   Excerpt from Vladimir Putin's speech on page 177.

65.   Second set of excerpts from Putin's speech on page 178.

66.   Quote about Donald Trump on page 179.

67.   Diamond CNN News, July 16, 2018, on page 179.

68.   Clay Travis and Buck Sexton, interview with Donald Trump, *The Clay Travis and Buck Sexton Show*, February 22, 2022,

Other Sources

Bale, S. Lawrence. "Gregory Bateson Cybernetics, and the Social Behavioral Sciences." 1998, 1-22. http://www.nabertha.com/Bale/lsable dop/cybemet.html.

Blow, Charles M. "Lie, Exploit and Destroy." *The New York Times,* February 8, 2018, https://www.nytimes.com/2018/02/08/opinion/trump-lie-mueller-investigation.html.

Bruni, Frank, and Ross Douthat. "Trump Can't Unite Us. Can Anyone?" *The New York Times,* October 30, 2018, https://www.nytimes.com/2018/10/30/opinion/trump-pittsburgh-polarization-midterms.html.

The Editorial Board, "Biden administration must declassify CIA torture program." The Boston Globe, November 8, 2021, A10.

Edsall, Thomas B. "The Moral Chasm That Has Opened Up Between Left and Right Is Widening." *The New York Times*, October 27, 2021, https://www.nytimes.com/2021/10/27/opinion/left-right-moral-chasm.html.

Edsall, Thomas B. "The 'Third Rail of American Politics' Is Still Electrifying." *The New York Times*, November 3, 2021, https://www.nytimes.com/2021/11/03/opinion/us-immigration-politics.html.

Epston, David, Michael White, and Kevin Murray. "A Proposal for Re-authoring Therapy: Rose's Revisioning of her Life and a Commentary." In *Experience, Contradiction, Narrative and Imagination: Selected Papers of David Epston & Michael White, 1989-1991*. Adelaide, Australia: Dulwich Centre Publications, 1991.

Fajarado, Remedios. Statement by the Representative of Wayuu Indigenous Rights Organization Yanama, La Guajira, Columbia. May 23, 2002.

Forrero, Juan. "Chávez Uses Aid to Win Support in the Americas." *The New York Times*, April 4, 2006, [insert URL or print page number].

Foucault, Michel. The Archaeology of Knowledge. New York: A.M. Sheridan Smith, 1972.Friedman, Steven, ed. *The Reflecting Team in Action: Collaborative Practice in Family Therapy*. New York: Guilford Press, 1995.

Freud, Sigmund. *The Origins of Psychoanalysis*. New York: Basic Books, 1954.

Freud, Sigmund. *Three Essays on the Theory of Sexuality.* Translated by James Strachey. New York: Basic Books, 2000.

Friedman, Thomas. "How to Stop Trump and Prevent Another Jan. 6." *The New York Times*, January 4, 2022, https://www.nytimes.com/2022/01/04/opinion/trump-jan-6-democracy.html.

Fromm, Erich. *Escape from Freedom*. New York: Avon Books, 1965.

Gergen, Kenneth J. *The Saturated Self: Dilemmas Of Identity In Contemporary Life*. New York: Basic Books, 2000.

Hebb, D.O. *A Textbook of Psychology*. 2nd ed. Philadelphia, Pennsylvania: W.B. Saunders, 1966.

James, William. *The Principles of Psychology*. New York: Dover Publications, 1950.

Kesey, Ken. One Flew Over the Cuckoo's Nest. Insert Publication City: Publisher, 1962.

Kristof, Nicholas. "Marching Toward a Massacre." *The New York Times*, January 16, 2019, https://www.nytimes.com/2019/01/16/opinion/sudan-protests-bashir.html.

Krugman, Paul. "Hate Is on the Ballot Next Week." *The New York Times*, December 29, 2018, https://www.nytimes.com/2018/10/29/opinion/hate-is-on-the-ballot-next-week.html.

Laing, R.D. *The Politics of the Family and Other Essays.* New York: Pantheon Books, 1971.

Levant, Ronald. *Masculinity Reconstructed: Changing the Rules of Manhood—At Work, in Relationships, and in Family Life.* New York: Dutton, 1995.

Madanes, Cloe, James P. Keim, and Dinah Smelser. *The Violence of Men: New Techniques for Working with Abusive Families: A Therapy of Social Action.* San Francisco, California: Jossey-Bass, 1995.

Martin, Jonathan. "Newsom's Anti-Trump Recall Strategy Offers Republicans a Warning for 2022." *The New York Times*, September 15, 2021, https://www.nytimes.com/2021/09/15/us/politics/midterms-california-republicans-newsom.html.

Maturana, R.R. "The Biology of Language," In *Psychology and Biology of Language and Thought: Essays in Honor of Eric Lenneberg,* edited by George A. Miller and Elizabeth Lenneberg,. New York: Academic Press, 1978.

McGinn, Marie. *Routledge Philosophy Guidebook to Wittgenstein and the Philosophical Investigations.* London, United Kingdom: Routledge, 1997.

Miller, James. *The Passion of Michel Foucault.* New York: Simon & Schuster, 1993.

Miller, Robert J, ed. *The Complete Gospels.* Sonoma, California: Polebridge Press, 1992.

Murray, Henry A. *Explorations in Personality.* New York: Oxford University Press, 1938.

Pagels, Elaine. *The Origin of Satan.* New York: Random House, 1995.

Piaget, Jean, and Bärbel Inhelder. *The Psychology of the Child.* New York: Basic Books, 1969.

"A Prayer for Tolerance." Unitarian Christian Prayer Journal, 2006. htriachristian.word press.com.

Sheinberg, Marcia, and Peter Fraenkel. *The Relational Trauma of Incest: A Family-Based Approach to Treatment.* New York: Guilford Press, 2001.

Shotter, John, and Arlene M. Katz. "'Living Moments' in Dialogical Exchanges." In *Dialog og Refleksion: A Festschrift for Tom Anderson on the Occasion of his 60th Birthday.* University of Tromso, Norway.

Wagner, Sarah. "Venezuela: Illiteracy Free Territory." *Venezuelanalysis.com*, April 21, 2005, https://venezuelanalysis.com/analysis/1079?artno=1427.

White, Robert, ed. *The Study of Lives: Essays on Personality in Honor of Henry A. Murray.* New York: Atherton Press, 1969.

CPSIA information can be obtained
at www.ICGtesting.com
Printed in the USA
BVHW011832141222
654260BV00018B/657